Heat 'Em Up
Survival of da Hood

By: Benjamin R. Perkins

I0163901

Copyright © 2008
 By Benjamin R. Perkins

All rights reserved under Good & Evil Publications in 2012,
St. Augustine, Florida. Bridgeport, Connecticut

 goodnevilrecords@yahoo.com

Library of Congress Cataloging-in-Publication Data

000-0810-4985-1111

Manufactured in the United States of America

First Edition

Just maybe you're thinking about being a dope dealer.

Shit, I'm not going to knock your hustle ladies & gentlemen, cause believe me I've been there before. But, explore your options. Weigh it all out. Is this life best for me, does it fit my profile? Most of all, can you do the time if you get caught? It's a lot of things that come with the dope game, which in this book. I did my best to cover all the aspects, such as murders, warfare, jackers, gold- diggers, cops, and the mufuckin' haters.

You can't forget who's winning the popularity contest these days. Yep, those punk ass snitches.

Choose your destiny, and stay focus. Cause no matter the lifestyle, you're gonna have haters. And though I changed my life, it's no question about it, will I do my best to strike at whoever's out to get me.

You got to get them before they get you. Nevertheless, some of you must learn the hard way. My man Thirst, in this book, was a young man with an old man's mind. Only eighteen years old, and wasn't with the foolishness anymore.

People seemed to not notice or understand, but he had ideas no one knew about. He replayed them in his mind all the time. He just knew he needed the money   to accomplish his goals. He decided after his early adolescence, that he wanted to work for it.

It was too much going on in the game for him. Meaning, he no longer found the excitement thrilling and captivating.

Though he knew a blessing lied ahead for him, there were times he thought he wouldn't live to see it.

Yet he kept the faith, and seemed to survive every time. It was his determination and motivation that gave him strength.

At all cost, he'd do whatever it takes to keep harm away from he and his family.

You'll enjoy this book.

Its fast pace, versatility, and mysteriousness, will keep you on edge.

Please note the contents may be offensive, and not suitable for young readers.

The Opening Event
<u>CHAPTER 1</u>
SCENE 1

It was a crisp cool breeze blowing throughout Kings County, New York. At 7 a.m. Thirst's alarm clock went off. His alarm was a boom box that echoed a jam that he had been waking up to for the past few weeks. It was Nas…. "woke up this morning, got yourself a….." But oddly, this morning Thirst didn't budge. He had done some overtime at his job the day before to help out his boss. Thirst was beat. It didn't help at all waking up to a blow to the head with a pillow by his younger sister. "Thirst, momma said get up and turn that radio down before she sends it to the garbage."

Thirst jumped up chasing Keisha out of his room yelling, "hit me again, I'm a break your neck." Keisha shouted, "Mom help, Thirst is trying to kill me. " Thirst slowly turned back towards his bedroom wiping his eyes, then gazed out of his window to see if he could determine the weather so he could know what he should wear this morning.

He reached under his pillow and grabbed his bible, which he just started sleeping with a couple of days ago, and set it on the nightstand nearby. He reached under his pillow again and pulled out his chrome 357 with a black rubber grip. He smirked then shook his head.
He had been sleeping with his gun for the past five years now.
This particular gun he just bought two months ago. He usually carries it when he is not going to work.

Thirst stood and placed the gun up on the top shelf in the closet in his bedroom. He strolled out of the room and went into the bathroom to wash up. Almost the very instant he went into the bathroom his younger sister, Keisha began banging on the bathroom door.

"Thirst hurry up, my ride will be here in a little while." "Keisha you know I use the bathroom the same time every morning. Why do you keep waiting until I get into the bathroom to have to use it."

"Just hurry up!" "I'll be out in a minute."

Meanwhile Sheila, Thirst's mom, is preparing breakfast. Thirst's younger brother Jaquince was sitting at the table waiting to eat. James, his dad is putting on his work boots in the living room. James said, "honey soon we will have a bigger house so these kids can have their own bathroom. Get out of this freaking jungle of Crown Heights and we will have a better place to live all together."

James started walking to the kitchen area. Sheila said, " Aw, James the Lord's will honey, the Lord's will!" They kissed briefly, and Jaquince had an icky look on his face, and then smiled. Thirst came out of the bathroom and Keisha pushed him to the side. She rushed in closing the door thinking Thirst was going to attack her. He just turned back around and went into the kitchen. "Hi mom, what's up pops?" "Good morning son", both parents said. Then James said, " don't be late for work Travis, all right? See you later", they all said, "See you later".

Travis is Thirst's real name. Sometimes his mother calls him T.R. the R is for Ramone. She would say "Travis Ramone Thurston, did you hear what your father said? You better hurry up."

" O.k. mom I'm taking this sausage and egg

sandwich with me." "Well it's your fault you have to eat on the run, taking your sweet time getting dressed." Thirst said, "Have a good day mom." and kissed her on the cheek, then said "See ya Jaq." "See ya Travis." Thirst's job was about three blocks away from the house.

At a steady pace he can get there in ten minutes, he has to be to work at eight O' clock. It was about six minutes to the hour when he made it downstairs. Thirst moved quickly.

At work he met up with his new friend Gordo, a pretty big Spanish guy he works with at the warehouse. "Hey, what's up my man?" "What's happening Gordo?" "Yo, I see the hot mommy over there checking you out again this morning." "Ha, Ha, Ha" they laughed. "Gordo you crazy, she's looking at you." "No, no, no my friend, look at her."

Thirst's breath froze " Yo, man your right, and she's actually looking attractive to me today. I don't know Gordo." "What do you mean? You don't like Latinas?"

"No it's not that, I just don't want to lead her on. Look I have enough problems. I have a bitch I can't trust, I need my own place, God knows I do. Slice's bitch ass always after me, always talking trash to me, and I'm broke as a joke."

" Wait a minute, wait a minute. Slice is still giving you a hard time?" " Yo, I'm through with that lifestyle, fuck Slice." Gordo began to nod then looked around.

"Yo, here she comes, but uh oh, so is the boss. " Gentlemen, may I ask you two to please at least put a little effort into your duties. These loads got to be out by lunch. Move it, move it, move it!" Then he walked away. Gordo said,

" Yo, Thirst I'll handle that, you go talk to her, man." Thirst and she became face to face within an instant.

" Hello, I'm Stephanie." "Hi Stephanie, look I'm just an average guy right now, have no time for relationships, I've got stress overloaded by the case loads. I don't mean to be rude, but maybe some other time o.k." She said "asshole", and walked away. Thirst shrugged and went back to work.

"How'd it go Thirst, huh?" "I told you Gordo,

I don't have time for that." Gordo didn't understand his words, so he shrugged it off and went back to work.

Scene 2

Lunchtime came, and routinely, Gordo and Thirst went out the back of the warehouse outside. Gordo reached in his pocket and pulled out a joint. Thirst said, "Yes sir. That's what I'm talking about. Good ole Mary Jane to ease the pain."

" Man, this is not Mary Jane. This is angel dust." Thirst looked crazy at Gordo. Then Gordo said, "Just kidding man, I didn't mean to almost make you shit your pants. Yo, Thirst it's Friday, so how about you come over and meet my family tonight, ay?" " Say Gordo, that sounds great man what's the occasion, though?"

"Nothing. I mean, ain't shit else to do. And you seem like an alright guy. I've decided I want you to meet my family."

"Alright, I'll be there." After a moment, Gordo said, "keep your head high Thirst, things WILL get better." "Sure Gordo, sure."

Scene 3

At 4:30 p.m., Thirst left the warehouse. He reached his block when he ran into Slice, Thirst's ex friend back in high school. "What up Thirst." "Look Slice, I don't have time for your games…."

"Listen muthafucka, all I said was what up. I know you don't want to be down. Make some real cash. Why? Cause you're a bitch that's why." Thirst swung and caught Slice in the jaw. Then he swung again and Slice went underneath him and slammed him to the ground. Slice stood up and kicked Thirst in the side, then knelt down beside him. "If you ever in your life, put you hands on me again, I'll KILL you, you understand?" Slice stood up and walked away, and jumped in his jeep. Thirst got up slowly. He knew how much Slice really hated him. He didn't trust Slice at all. He knew he murdered, and probably would have murdered him if it wasn't light out and everybody was watching.

Thirst made it to the apartment building he lived in on the third floor. It was a three bedroom, one bathroom apartment. Thirst went inside and went to his mother's bedroom.

" Hey mom, hey Jaq, where's Keisha?" " She hasn't made it in yet son. Your father called and said he would be working overtime tonight.
He said a water line busted in the city and they have to dig it up." " What you watching?" " The news. They're talking about the war. The time may be near, Thirst. We all just need to get our lives together." " I know ma, your right."

With that Thirst went into his room to find something to wear. He pulled out of his closet a pair of Coogi jeans with a jacket to match, along with a pair of blue and white Nikes. Then he went into the bathroom to wash up.

Jaq went into the living room and turned the TV on. He began watching cartoon network, when the phone rang. Sheila said, " I got it Jaq." Jaq wasn't even paying attention. "Hello", "Hi is this Mrs. Thurston?" "Yes it is.", "Good evening, my name is Dr. O'barto, from the Kings County Hospital. I have your daughter here in room 327."

"Oh, no!"

"No, listen ma'am, she's fine, she only suffered a few wounds and a slight concussion. I just wanted to make you aware that she will be staying here a few days. So if you would like to visit, please feel free."

"Thank you doctor, I'm on my way." She hung up the phone, "Thirst please hurry out, your sister's in the hospital." Thirst began to hurry, and got dressed quickly. Sheila told Jaq, "Hurry up put your shoes on son, we have to go see Keisha in the hospital."
At that moment Thirst came out, "You said Keisha, What happened?
"I don't know yet son, please just write a note for your father and tell him to get to the hospital as soon as he can." "O.k. mom." Sheila rushed off into the bathroom. She was out within minutes. They all rushed out of the apartment together, and went to the corner of the block to catch a taxi.

Meanwhile, the sexy latina Stephanie was walking up the block, and a white van pulled up beside her. She walked towards it and hopped in. "Took you long enough Peto. Did you do what Boss told you to do?" "Listen here girly, you're getting a little too hot for your own pants. Just do what your told now, sit back and be quiet." "Peto, I thought you loved me?" She said in a sly voice.

"Ha, Ha, you really funny you know that?" Peto said without a smirk. Stephanie didn't smile either. "O.k. I like you alright, but the only reason you're riding with me is cause of your looks, do you understand?" Nonchalantly she said "Yeah Peto, I understand." They made a right turn to take the Verrazano Bridge towards upstate New York.

Scene 4

James parked the car at the hospital and jumped out rushing towards the emergency room entrance. He met a receptionist, "Yes, I'm looking for my daughter, Keisha Thurston, the rest of my family should be here, too." " One second sir." She logged on to her computer and scanned the screen.

"Yes sir, she's on the third floor, room 327." "Thank you." James rushed to the elevator, once he arrived on the third floor he saw Thirst. He was speaking with a detective of some sort. James interrupted,

"What's going on?" The cop said, "are you the father of Keisha Thurston?" "Yes I am." "I was just explaining to your son about the accident that took place with your daughter." "Well explain it to me."
" We found evidence of what may have caused the accident. Nitroheliudrox, is a gas that does not need a flame to explode. Once heated up, the gas expands, then explodes. Traces were found in the tire of the vehicle that flipped over." "Flipped over!?! Whose vehicle!?!"

"Apparently it was her friend's car, the car she was riding in from school." "Where's Keisha, how is she?" James said panicking. "She's o.k. dad, just a few bruises." James's breathing settled a little.

"My daughter was in a car that flipped over?" "Yes sir, looks like twice. Whoever did this wasn't trying to harm them, but scare them, most likely. This has happened many times before, kids playing tricks on each other. But in this case, Miss Patterson, your daughter's friend, was turning a corner at the time her tire exploded. That's what caused the car to flip over." "How about Tasha? You know, Miss Patterson, is she o.k.?" "Yes sir, she's with her family. Minor bruises so she didn't have to stay. Keisha on the other hand has cuts the doctor would like to fix… and a slight concussion."

"Concussion!?! Look, I have to go see my daughter. Wait, do you have the bastards that caused this?" "No sir, I'm afraid not. No prints found as of yet. Officers have taken the car to our investigating center. We are going to continue to search for physical evidence." "Yeah."

James ran off towards Keisha's room. Thirst nodded at the officer, then followed after his dad. Keisha was smiling, didn't seem hurt at all. James showed a great relief when he saw her. He leaned over and kissed her on the forehead.

"How're you doing baby girl?" "I'm fine daddy." "Great, so lets go." Keisha laughed, and her mother said, "Not yet James, they want to do surgery to remove her scars. She doesn't want all those scars to be visible in her face. Besides she still has a slight concussion. We'll be home tomorrow night."

"I understand, so you're going to stay the night with her?" "Yea, my baby is going to need me here beside her tonight." "Ma", Keisha said, "I'm not a baby anymore."

"Right Keisha, anyway James I brought her and I a change of clothes and things with me, so we'll be fine." "O.k. dear. What about Jaq?" "I'm coming with you, dad." "Alright we'll see you young ladies tomorrow then, bright and early."

With that he gave both his wife and Keisha a kiss right below the temple. "Goodnight, come on Jaq. You coming with us, Thirst?" "Ugh, yeah, goodnight Keisha, goodnight ma. See you tomorrow."

They reached the parking lot when Thirst stated, "Pop, I think I'll stay over at Stacey's house tonight."

"Good idea son, then you can tell her about what happened with her sister."
"Yeah, mom tried to call her, but she wasn't home." "So I'll drop you at Stacey's house?"

"Well actually I'm going to take a trip to Shamika's house first, so I'll take the bus." "Alright son, see you tomorrow. Tell Stacey to come too." "Alright pop, see you Jaq." "Bye Travis."

<u>Scene 5</u>

A black Lexus jeep was parked outside a five story housing building. Inside was Slice and Shamika. "Damn that shit feels good bitch. Yeah, that's what I'm talking about." Slice began to spasm then released. Shamika kept sucking. "Hold up bitch. Ah…I said chill." "What's the matter daddy, you can't withstand these magic tonsils?"

"You're a fucking freak, you know that?" "What you say! Huh, you want more?" "Hell no bitch, you trying to kill me? Here, get this money and get the hell out."

Shamika smiled at Slice and jumped out of his ride. Slice peeled off, picked up his cell phone and hit one button. "Yo Pete, I'm on my way. Listen man, I'm on my way." He hung up the phone. Turned the radio up and pressed harder on the gas.

A city bus was pulling up to the curb. The doors opened. Then Thirst got off the bus and began walking up the block.

He made it to Shamika's apartment building and went up the stairs. When he reached her floor, he saw a chico coming out of her apartment. He passed him looking at him crazy, and chico did the same.

He knocked on her door, and she let him in. She said, "hey baby, I didn't think you were going to come see me. You haven't called me none today." Thirst didn't respond, he just sat down on the couch tiredly. Then looked at the ceiling.

"You're alright Thirst?" After a few seconds Thirst said, "I don't even know why I come over this bitch, anyway." "Don't start that shit Thirst, I'm not with your tired ass games tonight." "Me start shit? All I try to do is help you and your daughter like she's mine, and all you do is act like a fucking whore."

"Listen here muthafucka, you barely do anything for me or my daughter. So now that you wanna hear it, I'm not gonna front. I sell pussy!" "You nasty bitch. How could you? I ought to fuck you up."

"Sit down little boy, your coward ass ain't gonna do shit. Just like Slice is gonna fuck you up when he sees you." "What? You know about Slice?" "Your ex friend, yeah, I know. Well, I'm fucking him."

"O.k. bitch. That's how you wanna do it? This shit'll come back on your ass. Kiss Tiaja` for me." Thirst went out and slammed the door.

Meanwhile Slice pulled up on the set, "what up Pete?" "SLICE! Yo, my main man. I know I should've called you earlier, but shit just moving way too fast tonight.

And the bitches got them suckaz spending dollars like it's going out of style." "Yeah? Busy tonight, huh?"

Popping his collar, Pete said, "Well you know, Pete Ellis is a natural player in the game. And you, a fuckin genius. You got me working the field; you got the bitches making them suckaz upstairs in the Kitty Kat, buy ass and coke 'til they broke. Four look outs for each end of the block. Man, you're bad 'til death."

"Speaking of lookouts Pete, what the fuck is he doing coming down here." Pete turned around, "yo, what the fuck you doing nigga? I told you, if you want something hit me on the two way."

The lookout got close enough to Pete to slice his throat. Slice said, "what the fuck?" And instantly pulled out his heat. He shot the guy before he could even raise his gun. Then Slice got on the phone and called his main man Van Damage.

"Yo Damage, I need you to watch out for the 23rd for a few days. I'll make it beneficial to you…trust it." Then Slice jumped in his jeep and left.

Scene 6

Meanwhile, Stephanie and Peto were sitting in the parked van outside a pearly white mansion. "why are we leaving so soon Peto?" "Why do you ask so many questions?" "Well I never got to meet Xavier." "Don't worry about it bitch, just shut up." "Bitch? Oh hell no muthafucka, I ain't…." "Wait a minute, I'm sorry o.k. I'm sorry. Here, give me a kiss." He kissed her on the cheek. "Ah, Peto."
Then he started up the van and drove up to the gate, punched in a code and the gate opened. He drove out the gate through a pass, over hung and surrounded by trees, 'til he made it back to the road, which leads back to the city.
"I think I'm beginning to like that kid."
"Well, don't o.k. I got plans for us."
"Me too papi." Then she kissed him on the cheek as they took off down the highway.

Thirst made his way up to his sister's block. He saw a black Lexus jeep up ahead that resembled the one he saw Slice driving earlier today. As he got near his sister's house, he

noticed it was parked right out front. Thirst said aloud to himself, "I know damn well that nigga not seeing my sister."
He went up to the door and knocked. Stacey answered. "Who is it?"
"It's me." She opened the door, tightly wrapped in a nightgown saying, "who is me. Why you always saying it's ME? Like I'm supposed to know who me is. THIS is Brooklyn."

Thirst sounded a little uptight as he stated, "Well you know my voice." "Whatever, it doesn't matter…" "Where is he?" "Where is who, you idiot?" "The nigga that drives that jeep out there."

"None of your business. What do you want?" "Well I told pop I was coming over to stay." Stacey took a huff as is if she figured. Thirst continued, "and to tell you Keisha's in the hospital."

"What, what happened?" Stacey said worriedly.
"She was in a minor car accident. She and her friend Tasha." Stacey drew a slight breath of relief and bowed her head.

"Mom's been trying to call you, Stacey."
"I'm sorry. Come in Thirst. I know you know how to make yourself at home, 'til morning.

Eat up everything and fall asleep with the TV. on. We'll get up bright and early and go see Keisha." "Thank you Stacey."

"What's going on Stacey?", Slice stated. He came out of Stacey's bedroom and started hugging her around her waist. "What up Thirst?"

"You MUTHAFUCKA!" Thirst rushed towards him, then Slice pushed Stacey to the floor as him and Thirst began swinging at each other. Thirst caught Slice with a solid right beneath his chin.
Slice swung back with a left and hit Thirst in the temple. He seemed to daze him because Thirst staggered then fell. Stacey yelled, "No, stop it!" Slice stood over Thirst and pulled out a 44 magnum from his waistband and aimed it at Thirst's face. "No, please Devin. That's my brother, please."

Slice then lowered his aim, leaned down towards Thirst and slapped him thunderously with the pistol. Slice walked out of the house without saying a word.
"Oh my God, no. Thirst, are you o.k.?" Thirst shook his head slightly. He was badly bruised with a cut above his left eye. He got up slowly. Stacey escorted him to the bathroom to wash up. "I'll go get you an ice pack. There's some

peroxide and bandages in the medicine cabinet."

"Thanks."

Thirst washed his face and looked into the mirror. He shook his head. He was very upset with the outcome of that scenario. He put the bandage over his cut, and walked out into the living room.

Stacey handed him the ice pack. "I'm sorry about that Thirst. You'll never have to worry about that again. I didn't know he was like that." Thirst bowed his head and nodded. Then she said, "get some sleep bro. We gotta get up early tomorrow." She kissed him on the forehead and went to her room.

Thirst stood up to make a sandwich along with a bowl of Cheerios, and sat down in the living room. He grabbed the remote control from the coffee table and switched the channel to B.E.T.

Comic View was on. He watched it until he dozed off to sleep.

He woke up that morning with the sun beaming through the thin curtain, almost blinding him. He glanced at the clock above the TV. It read 7:58 a.m. He looked at the TV. It was Nas kicking down a chair in his "One Mic" video.

He sat up, then slowly removed himself from the couch and went towards the bathroom. He heard the shower running. Stacey was already up. He went and sat back down, then decided to make a bowl of cereal. Honey Nut this time.

He started eating then he heard the bathroom door open. "Hey Stacey, are my clothes still in the closet in the spare bedroom?" "Yeah", she said loudly so he could hear her from her bedroom. Thirst finished his cereal and went to find something to wear.

He decided on wearing True Religion jeans with a matching plaid shirt. He went into the bathroom, laid his clothes across the sink, and lifted the toilet seat to micturate.

Stacey knocked hard on the door and Thirst jumped. His urine went over the side of the stool. "God damn it Stacey."

"I wasn't finished Thirst, hurry up." Thirst got in the shower anyway and Stacey was pissed. "Don't try me Thirst." She soon realized Thirst wasn't coming out, so she went back to her bedroom to finish getting dressed. She was putting on her makeup when the phone rang. "Hello."

"Stacey, are you coming up here to see me?"

"Of course I am Keisha, I'm on my way out the door now, as soon as THIRST gets ready."

"Alright, see you in a little while then."

"Alright Keisha , love you." "Love you too." They hung up. Thirst was coming out of the bathroom and Stacey met him at the door with a punch to his forehead. "I said don't try me." "Stacey, I already have a headache." "Oh, I forgot…I mean, I'm sorry Thirst." "Are you ready Stacey?"

" Yeah let me just warm up a bagel and we'll be ready to ride." As she was warming up her bagel she asked, "are you still seeing that ho, Shamika?" "Hell no."

"As of when, just now?" "Well actually, I dropped her ass last night. Guess I finally got fed up with her shit. Especially after rumors revealed themselves to be true to me last night." "Damn. So you seen it with your own eyes?" "Yep." "That shit's gotta hurt." "Whatever. Are you ready?"

"Yeah, let's go."

They went outside and got in Stacey's car. A silver, four door Nissan Altima. Stacey's c.d. player began playing when she started the car.

It was "Gangsta Lovin'", by Eve featuring Alicia Keys. Thirst said, "You need to update your CDs sis." "Shut up boy, I'm on my old school shit right now."

Back at the house James decided to take the bus because the car had a stutter to it. It was a 1976, Lincoln Continental, cream colored with tan interior. He told his son, "we'll take ole Sampson to get a tune up when we get back. He's been good to me. It's time to give him a treat." Jaq laughed, "you treat that car like a baby dad." "Well, it deserves it, don't you think?"

"Yeah...I've been good too." "Have you really? I haven't even noticed. So, I guess you have been good son.
So, you want a tune up too?" "Nooo.." Jaq said laughingly.
"No, well what do you want?" "Ice cream! And a Spiderman toy!"
 "Alright, ice cream and a Spiderman toy it is." The bus pulled up and James finished,
"But first, let's pay Keisha a visit. Then we'll get the car fixed and take a ride by ourselves today." "Yay...thanks dad." "No problem, son.

Mastering A Disaster
Chapter 2
Scene 1

"Listen up. Now you all realize what I want to result from all of this." They all nodded their head and Xavier continued. "Stay on his ass until he reveals the prey."

There were eight guys Xavier spoke to in the large room, which he calls his conference room. They sat around a huge, oval, oak wood table.

"Do you all understand me? So make sure your boys continue doing what they suppose to do, and this thing will turn out perfect. Peto, where's the girl?" "Uh, sh-sh-she's downstairs boss." "Let me meet her." "Boss she's gonna do what she's told." "I said, let me meet her."

"Alright…boss." Peto left the room to go get Stephanie. Xavier was a real intimidating

guy. He was black and half Italian.
He stood about six feet four inches, and
weighed about two hundred forty pounds. He
was a bald and very muscular dude. Xavier
looked around to observe his guys.

They were a rough looking bunch, too. Four
were Spanish and four were black.

Pleased with the power he possessed with
having this crew, Xavier smiled grimly and left
the room.

Downstairs, Peto said to Stephanie,
"Xavier wants to meet you." Stephanie jumped
from the couch and said, "really?" Peto
grabbed her and said, "look, don't you do or
say anything stupid." He gazed into her eyes,
then she snatched from his grip.

Peto put his head down slightly and said,
"go up those stairs and make a left." She ran
up the stairs and Peto dropped his head in
sorrow.

Xavier met Stephanie on the second floor.
"Hello, follow me." He opened a door to a
room and they entered. "So, how do you like
Peto?" "Oh, Peto, he's cool." "Is everything
going o.k.?" "Yeah, things are swell."
"So what do you plan to do, as for the job?"
"Tie that little, young punk in a knot for you

papi." "Is that so?

And what do you plan on doing, as for me." "Whatever you want." Xavier looked down at himself, and then slowly back at Stephanie.

Stephanie went to her knees and unzipped Xavier's fly, and began to fondle him. Then she placed all she could fit of his manhood into her mouth. Xavier said, "yes, you're perfect."

Back at the hospital, James, Sheila, Stacey, Thirst, and Jaq were all visiting Keisha in her in-patient room. Thirst said, "glad to see you doing fine Keish, what time is surgery?" She answered, "they told mom around two o'clock, and that it'll take about an hour.

They also did an cat scan earlier this morning. The results came back about twenty minutes before you and Stacey arrived. I just have a slight bruise to the head, so I'll be able to come home today. They told me to just relax, don't do to much moving around, and stay calm. I should be released around five o clock."

"That's cool, can I get you anything?" "No, I'm o.k." "Well if you would all excuse me, I'm going to grab me a snack. Would anyone like to join me?"

They all said "no." Then James said as Thirst was leaving, "I never seen anyone eat so much

and don't gain a pound.
That boy needs some vitamins Sheila." Shelia
said, "He better buy him some, then." They all
laughed."

Down in the hospital cafeteria, Thirst
grabbed a tray and went along the line pointing
out to the servers what all he wanted on his
tray. The total came to about eight dollars and
sixty-seven cents. Thirst took his tray and sat
near the entrance to the cafeteria. He dug in.
He didn't notice when Dr. Cohen approached
until she announced her presence.

"Hello," "Uh, hello." Thirst had to clear his
throat. He was looking up at Dr. Cohen, and
amazed by her beauty. "Do you mind if I take
a guess at who you might be?" "Uh, no, not at
all. Be my guest."

"You mean, you're offering me to dine with
you?" "Please, yes have a seat." "My name is
Dr. Cohen, and you are Thirst, right?" "Uh,
yes how do you know?"
She laughed and said, "you resemble your
sister and mother so much, and your mother
just can't stop talking about you. Mrs.
Thurston is such a nice lady." "Uh, thanks Dr.
Cohen." It was silence for a moment then
Thirst said, "If you don't mind me asking, is
that all your going to eat?"

"Well, I try to watch my weight. The least fattening things I eat blows me up, and I mean fast."

"Wow, I wish I had your metabolism." "What metabolism? I don't have one." They laughed, she concluded, "I have to work out at least twice a week to maintain my figure." "Seems you do really well...concerning your health." Dr. Cohen smiled appreciatively. "Could you give me some health tips on gaining weight Dr.?"

"Sure. Well, you see, you have to...." "I was hoping we could possibly discuss it over dinner, that is if you're not busy." "Why Travis, are you getting fresh with me?" "I don't mean to be aggressive at all, I'd like speak to you more, a-about health tips. A-At your convenience of course." "Uh huh. Well, no I'm not busy. Dining out for a change does sound nice." "Yeah?" "So maybe I'll call you and let you know." Thirst was shocked, and pleased she wanted his number. "Alright, when could I expect to hear from you Dr. Cohen?" "How about eight o clock?"

Thirst nodded and Dr. Cohen said, "And please call me Destiny." "Destiny? Possibly my Destiny?" "We'll just have to see about that. Excuse me."

And just like that, she was gone. Thirst really hoped to hear from her tonight.

She looked as though she was around twenty-six, that's about seven years older than Thirst. Yet he was still very attracted.

Stephanie came back downstairs and said to Peto, "Are you ready? Boss wants us to make that pick-up." "Yeah." Peto said, looking at Stephanie strangely as they walked out the door of the mansion.

"What's the matter Peto?" "Nothings the matter, get in." They got in the van and left the mansion. Once they got on the highway Peto said, "I think I've fallen in love with you. Can't keep a straight head in this game if you're in love. Plus, I don't want nobody that will screw around on me."

Peto pulled out a 9mm with a silencer. "Peto, no." He shot her right square in the temple. She was dead.

Peto looking straight ahead began to cry. He slowed and made a left turn off the road, then headed down a path. "Got to find you a nice plot." He stopped the van then fired up a cigarette. He took a few puffs then threw it out the window.

He looked over at Stephanie's beautiful, but breathless body. He snatched her skirt off, then her panties.

Then touched her vagina. He noticed that she hadn't had sex. Then he screamed, "No, oh my god, no." He cried.

Scene 2

Meanwhile, Slice was out on the avenue of the of the 23rd. "Yo, Van Damage, what you think? You think you might like a job?" "Yo, Slice I told you, I got my own thing. I'm on some entrepreneur shit, too.

But say, I got to admit, this is a pimpin ass job. I guess I'll call it extra pay. But check it, you got to be here on time. Get me some fuckin relief. And remember, this shit is temporary, son." "I got it man.

Just keep your eyes open out here.
I feel something in the fucking air, man.

Some motherfucker's hatin' on Slice's money." "Don't worry Slice, everything is gonna be everything. And you can believe that." Van Damage said cocking his gun. Then Slice said, "I'll get back with you on the intravenous juice. Just hold it down for a moment, I gotta go see what's up with these bitches", Slice said looking at the time on his two-way. Then Damage said, "aiight money, be out." Slice said, "Peace", then jumped in his jeep and sped off.

Thirst was leaving the cafeteria, and got on the elevator to go back up to Keisha's room. Once he arrived on the third floor his family met him at the elevator. Sheila said, "I'm glad you're back, Thirst. Sit with Keisha until we get back. We're going to get something to eat." "O.k." "We'll be back shortly. Thirst went to Keisha's room. She was watching television. "What's up sis?" "Oh nothing. You know ma, dad, and Stacey was discussing what happened to your face." "You mean they noticed it?"

"Well, duh. Ma didn't want to mention it, I guess with all that's going on, plus the fact that she didn't want you to say 'don't worry ma I'm not a baby'. You know the band-aid definitely stands out, especially when they know it wasn't there last night."

"So, did Stacey say what happened?" "No. she seemed upset by it though. Ma thinks she knows something. She said she'd just ask you." "Oh boy." "What?" "I don't want to discuss it either." "Well, you best stay out of trouble Thirst, mom's talking about kicking you out if you're thinking of joining a gang or something." "A gang? Yeah right. Mom should know better than that." " Well, you know mom's getting older and the streets are

changing to her.
Besides who can you trust?" "Me of course, her first son."

" Well prove it. Continue to work hard and maintain responsibility. Better yet, move out." "Be quiet." "Just kidding." "Whatever, can't believe you're trying to school your big brother. And what do you know about the streets are changing. You better sit down somewhere."

Keisha started giggling. Thirst said, "I'm serious." "Just chill bro!" "Just chill?…" Thirst went over to Keisha and started tickling her feet. She started kicking and laughing loudly.

They were silenced by a tap at the door and the entry of Dr. O' Barto. Dr. O smiled at the two and said, "Excuse me good people, I decided to start the operation a little early to get you all home sooner, if that's o.k. with you Miss Thurston?"

"Sure, it's o.k. Thirst, would you tell mom and dad I'll be back shortly?" "Sure Keish." Dr. O'Barto smiled, then ordered his orderlies to come in and roll Keisha's bed out of the room to where they were going to perform the surgery. Thirst left the room to tell his family what was going on.

After speaking to his family about Keisha, he then said,

" Well, I'm gonna head back to the house. Just hang out, take a nap, and wait for you all to return with Keisha." They all said, "alright." Then Sheila said,

"Be careful son." "Okay Mom." Thirst then left the hospital. Once he got outside he placed his hands in his pocket. Then he felt something and pulled it out.

A half of blount. "Oh shit!" With that, he remembered he was supposed to meet Gordo's family last night. He pulled out his cell phone as he was walking to the bus pickup area, and dialed Gordo's number.

" Yo Gordo, what's happening man?" "Oh nothing Thirst, what's happening with you, man?" "Yo, I forgot to call you last night, so much drama man." "Yo, I'm sorry to hear that. Everything's alright?"

"Yeah, it's just my sister got in a car accident. She's fine, but I had to spend some time with her and my family. I'm just leaving the hospital now."

"Well, say man, how 'bout tonight?" "Well, actually Gordo, I think I might have a date." "Ho, aw, uh, oh. Mr. Lover Man. Knock 'em dead kid." "You know me Gordo. See ya Monday." With that, Thirst jumped on the bus.

Peto put the finishing touches on Stephanie's grave. He reached into his back pocket and pulled out a pint of Bacardi Dark. Poured some on Stephanie's grave and turned the bottle up until he emptied its contents. Peto wiped his face. He became teary eyed.
His cell phone rang back in the van. He rushed to it. " Hello."

" Peto, your boys just spotted our decoy. They're gonna follow him. Make sure he doesn't get hurt." "Aiight boss. Sure thing." " Where's Stephanie?"
"Oh um, she's sleeping boss." "Sleeping? Well, You let her handle the pickup. The guys are expecting her."

"Uh, alright boss." Xavier hung up. Peto grabbed his hair and started walking about nervously. Then he dialed a number on his cell phone. "Ay, nothing physical." Peto jumped in the van and backed out of the path.

Thirst got off the bus on 9th avenue. He decided to cross through the park to get to the apartment building, which was on 10th avenue.

As he walked he decided to fire up that half of blount he found in his pocket.

He lit it. "Ah, Mary, Mary, Mary." Suddenly he heard a gun shot.

The bullet apparently came near him because he heard it, and seen a spark fly from the monkey bars he was now standing by. Another shot, followed by another. He took off. He didn't know where the shots were coming from, all he know is they were aimed at him. But, why?

He made it around the apartment building and ran up the stairs. Thirst was breathing frantically. He ran to the apartment and put the key in to open the door. He went in and slammed the door behind him. Facing the door, he leaned on it trying to ease his breath. Then he began checking himself for bullet wounds. After not finding any, he turned around.

Once he turned to face the inside of the apartment he dropped the keys in amazement at what he saw. The house was ruined. Someone had broken in, and almost completely ram shackled the apartment. "Son of a bitch….son-of-a-BITCH!" Thirst went to the bathroom and washed his face. He looked into the mirror and shook his head. Then he

looked up and closed his eyes and said,
"Please God help us."

Not allowing misfortune to ruin what he
had planned to do for his family, Thirst went
into the kitchen and pulled out some spaghetti
noodles and sauce from the cabinet, along with
salt, pepper and oregano. He went to the fridge
and took out a pack of hamburger meat and
sausage.
He also pulled out a pack of corn on the
cob. He placed the items on the counter, and
went back to close the fridge.
He searched for a pan underneath the counter
and found one. He turned the stove on medium
and placed the pan on the burner.
"So, how you feeling Keisha?" "Okay,
thank you for asking Stacey.
Are you gonna come over to our house with us
for a little while?" "Sure. What's for dinner?"
"Oh darn. I'll think of something," Sheila said.
Then James said,
"No honey, don't worry about it, I'll handle
it. I actually have an Italian recipe in mind."
Sheila said, "Sounds good, what's in it?" "No,
no, no, I can't give up the secret." "Ah, James,
you're so crazy."
They were leaving the hospital. Down in

the parking lot Stacey said, "I'll follow you all to the house."

Then James said, "Uh, Stacey…can we catch a ride with you?" Sheila and Stacey said, " What?" Then James said, "Well, Jaq and I decided to leave the car and catch the bus over here." Sheila said, "You did what?" Then Jaq said, "No Dad, it was all your idea."

"Quiet son, no telling on your father. Honey, the car needs a tune up, so **I** decided to take the bus. Jaq and I will handle that tomorrow. Let's just enjoy having Keisha back with us." "That's a bet dad." Then Stacey said, "Well, pile in like sardines, I guess. One in the front, three in the back. That's not too bad. Let's ride."

Thirst had the food simmering. He turned the burners on low, then went to his bedroom. He noticed that it hadn't been touched by the bastard, or bastards. Then he walked to closet and then pulled out a black leather, long sleeved Iceberg fit, along with a black Gucci sweater.

He scanned the bottom of his closet until he found his black Tim's. Then he reached up and grabbed the Magnum from the top shelf of the closet and threw it on the bed, along with his outfit. He went into the bathroom to shower.

Peto was traveling through Queens. He decided to spin the van around right in the middle of traffic to head in the opposite direction. Then his phone rang.
"Hello. Yes, I'm on my way now boss." Peto looked deeply disturbed.

Thirst came out of the bathroom. Damp with a towel wrapped around the lower half of his body. He went into his bedroom and turned on his stereo. He set it to disc two, track three. The speakers ignited Busta Rhymes, "Baby if you give it to me…." He began bobbing his head to this funk, as he was getting dressed.

At that moment his family was coming in the door. Once they entered they noticed the living room, "Oh no!", they said. Then Sheila said, "What in God's name Thirst?" Thirst heard his mother and lowered the volume on the stereo.
Then came out of the room, "Ma." "T.R., what is this? And where's your father's car?" "His car? I don't know Ma. When I came home, the house was like this. I'm upset too." "Well, some thief must have broken in." "A thief is right, my car is not out there" James said.

Then Stacey added, "Let's just call the cops and see if they can find the car. And Ma, I'll help you get the house back organized."
Then Keisha said, "Um, something smells delicious." "Oh, thank you Keish, I did it for you. Well, for all of you."

Sheila said, "Really son, that was so kind of you." Then she hugged him and gave him a kiss on the cheek. Then James said, "Boy, you just stole my kiss. And my recipe, I can smell it." "Sorry dad."
They all laughed. Then Thirst said, "well everything should be about ready. If anybody wanna volunteer to set the table," Keisha said, "I'll do it!" "No way Keish, relax remember." Then Jaq said, "I'll do it Travis." "Okay, and who's gonna keep helping you reach the plates and the silverware? Better yet, I'll do it while you all go wash up."

Stacey was speaking with the N.Y.P.D. on the phone. Then she hung up. "Dad your car has been towed." "Towed, for what?" "Well, the dispatcher said they found it outside the building here on fire.
A huge blaze."

"What? Ah, forget it. At least the T.V.'s not damaged. Jaq, go turn the TV. on." Jaq went and turned the TV on. It was the news, a special bulletin.

It got Thirst's attention because he knows someone by the name, Stephanie Sanchez.

A news reporter spoke, "The N.Y.P.D. got an anonymous tip from a caller who reported a murder of a 25 year old woman, by the name of Stephanie Sanchez. The caller refused to identify himself nor how the murder took place, nor where the body is located.

He only told the officials, before hanging up, that they're going to have to find the body themselves, because he's the one that shot her."

Thirst's cell phone rang, "Hello." It was Gordo. "Yo man, did you hear what happened to Stephanie?" Gordo sounded upset. "Yeah that's crazy." "Damn right it is. You better not have done this."

"Gordo, have you lost your mind? I'm at home with my family." "Yeah, well I hope so, cause I'll tell the cops everything I know." "Gordo, chill man, I'm no murderer. I have enough problems, can't you understand. I don't take human lives." Gordo said, "Yo, I'm sorry man. She was beautiful, that's all."

Thirst heard a woman's voice in the background, "Who's beautiful? You've been

cheating on me motherfucker?" Then Gordo said, "No baby, no. I'm talking about the girl that got killed on the news.
 I used to work with her." "Yo, Gordo, I gotta go man, I'll see you at work." "Alright, peace brother." "Peace."

Thirst hung up the phone and sat with his family.

Shelia asked, "What's wrong son?" "Nothing. It's just so weird how I might have to go to work and not see that woman again." "What woman, son?" "The one that was just reported dead on the news." "Oh no." Then Stacey said, "Whoa, that's kinda deep."

Then James said, "Now what's the occasion? Why are you all dressed up?" "I was thinking about hanging out tonight for a little while. Listen to a little jazz, ya know?" "Sounds nice son, I would go with you, but your mom might get jealous." Sheila said, "No way, go, have a good time."
"Nah, besides you heard Thirst. I think he wants to be by himself."

Thirst had his head down when all eyes were on him. Then he looked up and said, "I got shot at on my way coming home today" "What?" they all said. Then James said, "And you're talking about hanging out?" "Well, I don't think the bullets were meant for me. I still ran though."

"See Sheila, we gotta get the hell out of Brooklyn. Like on the outskirts, like Stacey. I don't want my damn kids getting shot at. I'm sick of it." With that he slammed down his table napkin and went to his bedroom. Sheila went after him. Keisha said, "You'll be alright Thirst, I believe that." "Thanks Keish." Keisha got up and went to her parent's bedroom door. Jaq followed. Keisha knocked, "Ma, Dad". They faced her, and both walked to her and embraced her. Then Jaq got wrapped up in the hug, too. Stacey came to the doorway, then Thirst. They joined in a family hug. Thirst said, "Ah, so much love. This is truly beautiful guys." They all said, "Don't ruin it", and began hugging again. Then Thirst's cell phone rang.
Sarcastically he said, " Ah man," then "hello". "Hello. Is this Travis Thurston?" "Yes it is. And is this Destiny Cohen?" "Yes. Ha, ha, ha. Hey, I was able to get out of the office early today. Can we make plans to meet within the next half hour?"
"Sure, where shall we meet?" "Well, I can come get you if you like." "Oh, uh, sure.

That'll be cool." "Alright, great. I'll see you at seven." "Alright" "Bye." "Bye."

Keisha said, "Wait a minute. You have a date with Dr. Cohen?"

"Yes. Is something wrong with that?" "No. Just very shocking that's all. Not saying you're **ugly** or **broke** or anything." They laughed. She concluded, "Nah, just kidding bro."

Then Sheila said, "How did ya'll ever meet? You know, she's a really nice, young lady." "You know, she says the same thing about you, Ma." "Really. Well, you better be sweet to her. And don't have her hanging out in the hood either. She's not that type of lady." "Okay Ma, I know."

Thirst kissed her, then Keisha on the forehead, and walked out and went into the bedroom.

He decided to lay back on his bed and listen to Lauryn Hill, "When it hurts so bad", began to play.

Scene 3

Peto was back at the mansion. Having to explain what had happened. They were in the conference room at the table. Xavier stood up. He had a sword in a sheath that was hanging from his waist. "So…Where's my money, Peto?" He was walking around the table with his hands folded behind his back.
"I couldn't get it boss." "What do you mean you couldn't get it? The girl is supposed to get it. Where is she?" "She's dead boss." "She's dead? What happened?" Peto hesitated, and began to cry. "She was my girl. Not yours boss. I cared for her." "Listen muthafucka. Fuck all that. What the fuck happened?" "I.I.I killed her god damn it." Xavier looked very upset. Then calmed his expression.

He walked up to Peto and patted him on the back. "You're with us… standing strong that is, but you fell weak." Xavier drew the sword without Peto noticing. "So you must leave us. Hah yah." "Ah", Peto screamed.

Xavier sent the sword through the back of Peto's chair. He died immediately. Xavier pulled the sword out of Peto's back swiftly. Then he handed the sword to one of the goons to be cleaned. He ordered the rest, "Go get my money. They'll be expecting you."

The sun had just hidden itself behind the horizon. Thirst jumped up and looked at the clock. It was 6:52. He got up off the bed and went into the bathroom quickly to wash up after his nap. He told his family he was leaving, grabbed his 357 and his cell phone and went outside.

By the time he made it outside and down the stairs, a red Navigator with tinted windows pulled up and stopped. Thirst stood observing. Then the passenger window came down and a voice said, "Do you want a ride?"

Thirst leaned to look in and saw Destiny's face, then smiled. Then made his way to the vehicle.

Destiny lowered the volume on the c.d. player. She was listening to a song by Mary, Mary. Thirst opened the door, sat down in the

Navigator, and closed the door behind him. Destiny said, "Your door is still open. You can slam it. It won't break."

Thirst smiled and slammed the door with a little more effort that time. "So, where are we headed?" Thirst said, "Well, I was thinking perhaps *Miracles* would be a nice spot for us to chill. All they play is jazz, soul, and some R&B. Always a live band, including table service." "That sounds perfect. Where to?" "25th and Madison. Hey, what're you listening to?"

"Oh that's a Gospel c.d., Mary, Mary. Have you ever heard of them?" "Yeah, but I never heard any of their songs. Turn it up." She did while saying, " This one's my favorite." "Yeah. It does have a beautiful melody."

"Doesn't it? It pulls you in, so you can't help but feel it." They listened to the song. Thirst started patting his thigh with his hand and moving his head to the rhythm.

Up ahead he noticed *Miracles*, but there was no place nearby to park. He said, "Drive up to the next block, there's no where to park here." She found a place to park at the next block, and began to show off her paralleling skills. Thirst smiled. They got out and Destiny appeared to feel the chill of the air through her thin jacket.

"Come here, you look cold", Thirst said. He wrapped his arms around her, and she said, "Thank you."

They made their way to the entrance of the club, where the doorman gave them a table number. They seated themselves and within minutes they were greeted by a waitress.

The band was playing contemporary jazz so the waitress had to ask loudly, " Can I get you something to drink?" Thirst asked Destiny, "What are you having?"

"Well, a virgin Pena colada would probably fit the mood, what do you say?"

"Well, daiquiris are not my style, and I don't drink virgin liqueurs…" "You could drink if you like. I'm driving." Immediately Thirst said, "A virgin Pena colada and a Courvoisier on the rocks." The waitress said, "Coming right up." "This is a pretty, nice spot Travis. Is this where you bring all your girls?" "Slow up baby girl. I felt this would be a special spot for us, and that's the first thing that comes to your mind during this occasion? Please baby, don't ruin the moment." "Sorry."

"No need, let's just have a good time." They watched the band play. Then Destiny asked, "So what do you do, Thirst?"

"I work at Shopper's Express in the shipping department. I just started there about three weeks ago. Other than that, I lounge at home in my room, or hangout at the sports pub sometimes. Yeah, it's a pretty dull life. But, I got this constant feeling that it's gonna pay off eventually."

"You know Thirst, I've been feeling the same way. Like a change is coming for me."
"Really? Could it be you and I?"
"I don't know, but to be honest, it feels like it. Look, it's uncommon for a woman to reveal information like this to a man so soon." The waitress brought the drinks. Destiny began taking a sip.

Then Thirst said, " So, you're just being honest, right?" Destiny responded, gazing into Thirst's eyes, "Yeah. Maybe it's something about you." Destiny shook out of her gaze and said, "We'll just have to see." Thirst smiled at the comment.

The waitress came back with some plates, and a tray of hors d'oeuvres for them to choose from. Different waitresses always come through with different hors d'oeuvres each time.

Scene 4

'My name is Slice/ I ain't nothing nice/ going all out/ roll the dice/...I want it all/ fuck the price....' Slice and his boy Truth were rolling through the city discussing the business. Slice's song was echoing in the background from the c.d. player.

"I feel the heat is on my nigga. Always got the fuckin' haters cause I got the money. But, I'm a show them bitches. I don't give a fuck. Killed my mufuckin' nigga, Pete, in cold blood. Them bitches gotta pay." "Who man? Who are you talking about?" "You know what, I'm sensing some fear over there in that seat. Yeah muthafucka, don't shake your head." "Listen, I'm not trying to die for your ass."

Slice hit the breaks quick. "Say word, nigga?" He pulled a gun out and aimed at Truth's head. Truth said, "Listen nigga. I'm Truth nigga."

Then Truth broke down a little and said again, "I'm Truth nigga. We went to high school together....alright, show me who it is and I'll get 'em."

"Nigga, I don't know who it is." "What the fuck? Listen man, I can't risk my life like that for you. I got a family, now." "Oh yeah nigga...you CAN die for me." Slice pulled the trigger. Truth's brains splattered on the window in the Lexus jeep. Slice got on the phone. "You, meet me at the spot. Gotta take out some trash." Slice turned up the radio and mashed the gas.

Back at the club, Thirst and Destiny were preparing to leave. Thirst reached in his pocket and left a tip. He grabbed his jacket from the back of the chair and laid it across his left arm. Then with his right arm, he interlocked arms with Destiny as they strolled out of *Miracles.*

Outside, he wrapped the jacket around Destiny. Then they headed the direction where the vehicle was parked. "I had a really wonderful time Thirst. It's been a long time. Thank you." "No, I thank you Destiny, for a wonderful evening." "I wished it could have lasted longer, but I do have to get some sleep. I have to go to church tomorrow. I had to skip the last two Sundays, due to work."

"It's o.k. I believe we'll have many more outings together to make up for this brief, but pleasant moment." Destiny smiled at that, and unlocked the doors to the truck. They both got in and the Navigator drove off.

At the spot on 23rd Ave, Van Damage was on post smoking a cigar. He stood about 6'2",235 pounds solid. He was a real mean looking dude. So was Slice. But, Slice gave Damage much respect. Slice pulled up beside Damage, "yo, meet me around back of the Kat house." Slice drove off. Damage strolled across the street towards the Kat house. Once they met behind the building, Slice jumped out of the jeep and explained to Damage what had happened.

"Whatever Slice. You fuckin' trippin' man. You know I'll help your ass, but you gotta stop doing crazy shit like this. Look at you. Give me that fuckin' bottle." Damage snatched the bottle of Hennessey from Slice. "I know Damage, man. Just a lot of fuckin' stress."

"Stress? Man you're probably the only young nigga in New York with the kind of money you got. And you're stressin'? Look, how about you take a vacation, you and the woman you like…what's her name?" "Stacey." "Yeah, yeah, let me run the spot 'til you get back." "Hay, I don't know man. I don't think she even likes me that much…We'll see, Damage. I'll think about it."

The Navigator pulled up in front of Thirst's apartment building. "Travis?" "Yes, Destiny." "Go to church with me tomorrow?" "Sure." "Great. I'll be here around 10:30 sharp." "Alright!"

They gazed into each other's eyes. "I would love to…but not tonight, Travis." "Me too…I mean, I understand. Goodnight, Destiny." "Goodnight, Travis." With that, Thirst exited the truck. He made his way up the stoop, and waved Destiny off. She tapped the horn in response and drove away. He watched her drive away, then turned to place the key in the door to get into the building. Then he heard two cars doors shut behind him. He turned around and saw a black limo with two guys standing outside of it. A man on each side of the limo, and they were facing him.

One of the men called out, "Mr. Thurston." "Who wants to know?" "Uh, how about my little friend…now get over here." Thirst noticed they had their guns drawn on him now. "GET in...I said GET IN!"

Thirst walked down the stoop, as one of the guys opened the door, walked up to Thirst, grabbed him and nearly tossed him in the back seat of the limo. They jumped in after him. These guys were huge, like linemen from the Giants. They wore black suits with bald heads. The limo drove off, and one of the goons handed Thirst a black tie. "Here, cover your eyes with this." "I don't wan...uh.." One of the goons elbowed him hard in the gut. He slowly got his breath back. "Around your eyes...NOW!" Thirst tied the tie around his head and pulled it up over his eyes. "Now, just sit back and relax. It'll be over soon."

Destiny couldn't help but look in her rear and side view mirrors, and notice that the same car had been following her for the longest. So she decided to keep making turns. Whoever it was must have realized she noticed them trailing her, because they finally turned the opposite direction at the intersection. Destiny was slightly relieved, and started to head home.

The limo was pulling up at a mansion. They uncovered Thirst's eyes, then jumped out of the vehicle and said, "let's go."
Thirst got out, then one of the goons grabbed his arm and pulled him along. They got up to the door of the mansion and went inside.

Thirst was too upset to be fascinated by the beauty of the place. They tugged him along, all the way up the stairs. They reached a door, Thirst noticed, that read <u>Conferee Room</u>. They went inside where there were many chairs surrounding a very large table. They made Thirst have a seat, then they sat in each chair beside him, nearly smothering him. Nothing happened for a moment, besides the silence. No one said a word. Just the three of them in this very large room, sitting together like the place was packed with guest. Thirst grew weary. Anxious even. It became nauseating. Then the door came open. Thirst looked up and saw a tan colored man enter the dim lit room.
He noticed the man was tall and built, with long, jet black, silky hair.

The man spoke. "Mr. Thurston..." Not amazed that these people knew him anymore, Thirst just listened. "I understand you know someone by the name of Devin Dumas." "Slice?" "Yes…Slice. He's an EX-friend of yours, correct?" Now Thirst was amazed. "How'd you know that?" At that moment, the door opened again. And another fellow appeared from behind it. He was about 5'10", 240 pounds. Then Thirst recognized who it was. "Gordo? What the hell is going on?" "Hello Thirst, old buddy."

Xavier spoke, "Gordo's been helping us help you, so you can help us." "What the hell do you mean? No one's been helping with shit. What the hell is this? Let me out of here…Gordo, I thought you were my friend, man." "Just listen to the master, pally."

"Mr. Thurston, Slice is our problem. Meaning yours and mine. We've been watching, and we know what he's been doing to you, and to us.
We've got to stop him before things really get out of hand." "So, what do you need with me? Seems you got all the manpower you need." "All you got to do is get him to stick around in one spot long enough so we can nail him." "You mean, so you can kill him?"

"Of course. Why not? So we can prevent these things from continuing to happen to us.

Slice is dirty, you know. I'm trying to run a legitimate business. I can't have him constantly causing destruction around the place, every time he gets upset."

Thirst was focused his eyes as to try to understand, then he dropped his head.
"Hey…don't worry kid. It's ALL going to pay off in the end.
Just whenever you see him you call me, o.k. Here, here's my number. Now WE'RE friends. But let no one see this ever, understand?! Now after you call me and tell me where he is, stall him. Talk to him for a while, o.k.?" "Look, I don't know. I know he's done some horrible things, but I can't have him murdered."
"Listen kid. No more games, DAMN IT. Your LIFE depends on it." Thirst became fearful. Thinking not only of his life, but his family's.
Xavier continued. "Now you either help us, or die. Your choice. Go show him what I mean boys." The two goons on each side of him pounced up as if they've been waiting for this opportunity. They jacked Thirst up quickly and took him out of the room.
"Gordo, let them know, thirty minutes, then let him get some rest.
He should have some sense in him by

morning. Then get his sorry ass out of my house." "Yes sir." Gordo immediately left the room. Xavier fired up a cigar. Puffed once. Then a peaceful look appeared on his face.

Scene 5

It was about 10a.m. The sun was shining bright in Brooklyn. On 10th Ave. Thirst was getting shoved out of the back of a limousine, that immediately sped off.

Thirst slowly picked himself up off the ground. He began to head up his block towards the apartment building where he lives. Something was piercing his side.

He stopped walking and reached in his waistline and pulled out the 357. He palmed it and angrily shook his head at it. Then threw it in the nearest gutter. He started walking again when his cell phone rang. "Hello." "Thirst?" "Shamika?" "Yes. Thirst I'm sorry to bother you. Man, I'm fucking up. I'm fucking up bad."

Shamika was crying. Thirst said, "What is it Shamika?" She sniffled, "I'm on drugs Thirst.

I fuckin got sprung out on this shit. I don't think I could love Tiaja` like she needs to be loved.

Please, come and get her Thirst, please."
"I'll be right there Shamika.

Give me a little time, okay?" "Okay." They hung up.

Thirst noticed a lot of commotion up ahead. Police cars and fire tucks. It appeared to be right out front of his parent's apartment building.

Thirst looked nervous. He started running. He noticed his family and other families outside the building. It was on fire. Keisha saw Thirst and she ran to meet him. They met. "Thirst", she hugged him tightly. "Oh my God, Thirst. We barely made it out. It's still some people trapped inside."

Thirst didn't speak. "If it wasn't for someone banging on our door yelling 'fire', we wouldn't have made it. It started on the top floor…This is crazy."

She began crying. Then Thirst grabbed her to hug her. Sheila, James, and Jaquince noticed Keisha was over talking to Thirst. They walked over slowly. "It's okay Keisha. Everything's gonna be okay", Thirst said. When the rest of the family made it over they all hugged each other.

Sheila and Keisha were sobbing. James intervened. "We'll just see if Stacey doesn't mind us staying at her house for a few weeks. At least 'til we can establish another residence." Sheila said, "but James, we lost everything." "Don't worry about it. We can replace those things. And besides, we were sick of this neighborhood anyway." "But, I don't think we should just go barging in on Stacey like that. She probably wants to be alone."

"Sweetie listen. Only a few weeks, okay? I'm sure our own child wouldn't turn us down in such a situation." "I guess you're right, dear. I just hate to be a burden on her. She's worked so hard to get what she has.
And she still has one more year in law school." "Well sweetie, we'll work something out. I'm more than positive."

James held his wife close at that moment. Thirst placed his hand around Jaquince's shoulder, while Keisha was still hugging him with her head down. Neither Thirst nor his family seen Destiny pull up.

She was all dressed up for church this morning. As she approached she asked, "Is everyone alright." Keisha said, "Dr. Cohen,…

Oh this is terrible!" "What happened?" "We were alerted by someone banging on our door yelling fire. We came out and the whole top of the building was on fire. People are still inside."

"Oh, no. The firemen haven't brought anyone out, yet?" "I don't know. I'm really not sure. I've just been standing here praying for them the whole time." The firemen were still hosing down the   building, though the flames seemed to   have depleted.
Destiny said, "Is there anything I can do to help?" Sheila said, "Please doctor, if you could give us a ride to my daughter's house, I would really appreciate it."
"I would love to."
They all got in the Destiny's vehicle, with Thirst sitting on the passenger side.

Sheila said, "I hope everyone made it out of there safe. They said some people were trapped on the third floor. Please God, protect them. Protect they're souls." She began sobbing, as James held her close.

At the 23rd, Slice was counseling Damage about the business. Damage was leaning against his car listening as the speakers pump 50 Cent's "Jump Off". "See, I know it's some muthafuckaz hatin on mine, so I gotta stay prepared at all times.

Blaze them muthafuckaz like an inferno. The pay will be proper, Damage. You'll be successful fucking with me."

"Yeah, I know Slice. But understand me, I'm not here to do no cleaning. I'll handle the security, make sure the order is in on time, but I'm not here to play Magnum P.I. and find out who your adversaries are.

Now, if you find them we'll trap 'em. The Van Damage, will make war on their bitch ass."

"As of right now, I don't know who the fuck it is, but…" gunshots rang from a black Mazda.

Slice and Damage ducked down behind a car, pull out their guns and fire back. The Mazda sped off. Slice and Damage got up looking around, brushed themselves off, and headed towards the *Kitty Kat*.

Slice said, "I swear to God, yo, I'm a find them muthafuckaz and the shit's curtains!" As they entered the Kitty Kat, Deleisha was sitting at her desk, Slice's receptionist and secretary type bitch. Slice said, "You, Deleisha, you know what to do. The cops are certain to come here asking questions once they find out shots were fired in this area again." Deleisha was nodding her head with a sly, smirkish look, knowing she was on point.

"I'm going out the back here. If you need anything hit me up, Dee." Slice and Damage left out the back entrance of the Kitty Kat. Hit the button on his key ring to unalarmed and unlock the doors to his pearl white Jaguar. They jumped in and peeled off fast. Going across the Geo Bridge, with Wu-tang coming through the speakers of the Jag, Slice said, "You wanna hit the studio wit me?"

"Yeah let's see what's up with Mix. That's the nigga that's been keeping me focused all this time. You know, I don't be with that rappin shit. But, that's still my nigga." Slice then responded, "Hell yeah. Without Mix and the music, I probably would've BEEN dead." Damage looked over at Slice with an evil, but questioning expression.

Slice said, "What nigga…What? Why the fuck you look at me like that?" "Just keep a clear head nigga. You're moving fast without thinking. This shit wouldn't be happening if you had your shit in tact."

"What the fuck you mean, Damage?" Slice asked in an angry tone.

He went on, "How am I supposed to have control over who's after my stash, when I don't even know who it is?" Damage implied, "Maybe if you'd look, you'll find. You ever thought about setting traps? Have you ever thought about anything, Slice?"

"Yes Damage, what the fuck man, are you with me or what, man?" "I already told you. I'll back you 100%, but the dirty work is out. I got my own shit to attend. Only because you're my nigga, I'm willing to go this far for you." Slice hissed, and began angrily bobbing his head to the music, speeding on in the Jag.

Thirst said, "thanks for bringing me and my family over to my sister's house. I hope…" "Listen Travis, it's o.k. Anything you or your family needs, I'm willing to help out.
You all are great, and I understand going through tough times. I've been there myself many times before. I just thank God for how he's blessed me. Now, I can help others." "Cool Doc, but you don't have to do that…" "Travis Ramone Thurston, you are my friend, o.k.?"

Thirst just sat there trying to search her thoughts for a moment, then said, "Yeah?" She said, "Yeah." she paused for a moment then replied, "Thirst. Do you know where I live?" "No, why you ask me that?" "Well, someone left this laying on my doorstep." She handed over an envelope, sealed with "Thirst" printed on the outside, to him.

He examined it for a moment, then opened it. "Well, what is it?" She said.

Thirst seemed astounded when he began to flip through the bills and saw nothing but hundreds. "Oh my, Thirst. That's a lot of money." Thirst was surprised, too. Then even more surprised when a thought came to his mind. He released the money and it fell to the floor of the Navigator.

"What's the matter Thirst? Is something wrong?" "Just put it like this: I had a long night last night. We need to talk." A look of awe appeared on Destiny's face as she studied Thirst, then glanced back at the road..

"How about we go to my house and have breakfast? Can we talk then?" Thirst said, "yeah, that's cool." Thirst was angry, but concentrating deeply on what he should do next.

Meanwhile, detectives were confronting

Deleisha. "How are you doing Miss? I'm Detective Culpepper, and this is my assistant, Detective Stevenson.

We're investigating in this area and we would just like to leave our cards in case you've seen anything suspicious going on around here."

Deleisha was shaking her head slowly as if not wanting to speak to the lawmen. "Here's our cards anyway Miss…" looking around he went on, "uh…do you mind if we have a tour of the place you have here?" "I think you ought to be on your way gentlemen. You've already done what you've JUST came to do. I have your number, good day." The detective nodded briefly then, looked up.

His eyes were fixed on a surveillance camera for a second before he let out a sigh of humor. He then looked back at Deleisha with the same sour grin then turned to leave. As soon as they left, Deleisha called Slice to inform him of what all just happened.

At the studio, Slice was in the booth spitting off lyrics, when the music stopped. Slice said through the mic, "What the fuck's wrong now, man? Damn." Mix said,

"Deleisha's on the phone nigga. She said, 'get your ass here. It's important.'"

Slice snatched off the headphones and went out to get the phone, "Yeah……Uh um….Alright…Oh yeah…alright decent baby, love." He hung up the cell and headed back to the booth. Damage called after him, "What's up Slice?"

"I'll holla at you in a minute, Damage." He shut the door behind him, grabbed the headphones, and yelled in the mic, "Music!" Damage leaned over to Mix, who was pressing the buttons to bring forth the music, "I think that niggaz losing it." "Yeah. I noticed. He'll be alright though. I'll back him to the fullest on whatever."

Back at Destiny's house, Thirst got a tour of her bedroom. After she had came out in a change of clothes, "I want to show you my paintings" she said. Destiny took Thirst's hand and guided him past the threshold of her bedroom. "I figured maybe you should relax a little before you tell what's on your mind. And this is just the painting to do it." "Damn…it's beautiful." "You like it?" "Hell yeah!" Thirst seemed to be getting high from its beauty. "I painted back when I was in the 11th grade. My grandfather taught me about the magic of artwork. It's like music. It soothes you." "Yeah, it's truly amazing."

Thirst leaned back on the headboard of Destiny's bed, sitting upright gazing at the painting. She watched Thirst for a moment then sat down beside him. Then he turned to face her, then spoke. "I have to get my daughter." "Your who? Your mother said she didn't have any grandkids."

"Well, it just happened." "What are you talking about, Thirst?" "I had this girlfriend. We broke up weeks ago. But, her daughter…I got really attached to her. Anyway, Shamika called this morning and told me she couldn't take care of her anymore."

"Oh no, that's terrible, but very kind of you, Thirst." "So, she wants me to come get her." "What're you gonna do Thirst?" "The best I can." Destiny had a look of concern on her face, and Thirst said, "Tiaja`." "What a pretty name."

"Yeah it fits her. If you could take me to get her, I would appreciate it. I guess I'll, stay over at Stacey's…" "No Thirst. You can stay here." "Well, Dest, I don't think…" "On the couch." "Cool." She was smiling graciously at Thirst. Then he broke the ice on what really had him down.

"I think I've been inducted into this mob. I believe that's where all this money comes from." "What?" "Yeah. Uh. They want me to set up an ex friend of mine." "No Thirst. That's crazy." "Tell me about it. I can't do that. I'm not gonna do it. But at the same time, I don't know what I'm gonna do.''

"What's this all about?" "I don't know. I think they're jealous of Slice. And the one guy I thought I could trust, he's down with those dudes. I work with him……not anymore…I gotta call Slice. We ain't cool, but I would have nothing to do with his death, unless he was trying to kill me. I thought he was at first. But I figured it out. It wasn't him at all. It's gotta be them. Trying to get me, to kill Slice."

He reached for the phone, then remembered his manners, "May I use your phone?" "Sure." "Tonight, I'll make sure it's not, Slice. Then find a way to get those upper class hoodlums off MY back." He dialed Slice's cell. Nodded his head in appreciation that he still had the same number. The music went silent again. Slice looking angry held his tongue. Mix said, "Your celly nigga." Slice snatched off the headphones and tossed them to the side, heading for the door.

Scene 6

Xavier was entering the conference room, in the event to have a meeting with Gordo. "Gordo. Did you take care of the clothes he's wearing?" "Yes sir. I did." "Good. Hopefully he doesn't change anytime soon. The rest of his things were destroyed in the fire. I'm certain he's gonna plan a meeting with Slice soon to get his worries over with. I want you to watch him closely. The first chance you get...rip Slice to pieces." Gordo nodded his head with a look of fear in his eyes for Xavier. Xavier began to chuckle, then outright laughed devilishly.

Thirst was hanging up the phone with Slice. Destiny said, "So what's up?" "He said to meet him at the Eastside Café, at six. He's probably thinking I'm ready to work for his dumb ass, but he's in for a much bigger surprise." Thirst sighed, then went dazing as if in thought with a hint of depression.

Destiny intervened, asking, "Thirst are you okay?"

He said nothing, so Destiny sat closer to him and wrapped her arms around his shoulders. She looked upon him for a moment, then kissed him on the cheek. That seemed to break his spell. Because he immediately turned and looked into her eyes.
Passion seemed to overtake him as he returned the kiss, to her lips. That same passion must have overtaken Destiny because the kissing continued, but more deeply.

Tonguing each other, their hands were thoughtlessly fondling each other's body and face, and hair.

They fell back on the bed. Thirst rolled on top of her, still kissing her and fondling her breast. All of a sudden, he stopped. Looking into each others eyes he asked, "Do you want me Destiny?" she replied, "Yes."

Thirst was motionless for a moment as Destiny hesitated to say, "But I feel we should wait…just a little while. I always wanted to wait until I get married." "You mean…" Destiny nodded silently, saying, "Yes."

Thirst began to blush and say, "Whoa", he leaned down and kissed her on the forehead, and said, " I knew you were special, but how could I be so blessed to be cared for by you?"

"Because you're special. Although, I should be the one asking you that question." She continued, "Listen Thirst, we're not gonna take it so slow that we'll both get bored. So we're just gonna go with the flow. How about we go get Tiaja`, then grab a bite to eat."

She was hopping up from the bed. Thirst was smiling up at her. She said, "Come on." Thirst got up, then they left.

As they were riding Thirst began telling Destiny about his talk with Xavier. "He seemed like some godfather type. The other dudes in there seemed to look up to him."

Destiny listened, "Come to think about it. That warehouse must belong to him.'' "What warehouse, Thirst?" "The one I work at." "Oh no" "Yeah, things did seem kinda funny around there. The boss is always watching and looking over your shoulder. The place is loaded with cameras." Thirst thinks back to a time he was at work.

He was loading a truck, and from a box, a

powdered substance leaked from one of the cracks, and as usual the boss was right there and told him to leave it. He told Thirst to shut the door of the trailer and he'll have somebody come clean it up.

"I've been helping them ship drugs all across the country." "Oh my God ,Thirst, you can't go back there." "Trust me, I've planned not to. The only guy I've come to trust has been with them the whole time, to get at me to get to Slice. And this filthy two hundred grand, I'm thinking about throwing this shit in the river." Thirst wiped his forehead, clearly upset, shaking his head in disgust. Destiny said, "maybe it's still a blessing..I mean your family could really use it." "Yeah, but at the same time you can't receive blessings from the devil, right?" Destiny slowly nodded her head and glanced at Thirst. "Pull over there."

Destiny pulled over towards the curve and stopped the vehicle. Thirst opened the door and said, "Just one second." He got out and closed the door. He walked over to a man lying on the ground and gave him a stack of money. He didn't wait for a response, he turned around as if looking for someone.
He saw a young lady carrying a small infant. She seemed very poor and distressed. He

handed her a stack of money.
Thirst stopped for a moment because she began yelling, "Thank you God, I love you!" Thirst got back in the truck.

"Oh, Thirst, that was wonderful." Destiny hugged and squeezed him, and kissed him on the cheek about five times. "Okay, it's not such a big deal. I had to do that."

"You're so beautiful", she said sexily and gazed at him for a moment. "Okay Destiny, cut it out. Are you trying to start something here?" "Nothing I can't finish." Thirst had to catch his breath and clear his throat, "OOh."

She laughed at him and drove away.

Surprise Surprise
Chapter 3
Scene 1

"You sure you don't mind taking her with you?" "No, not at all Thirst. We'll be fine. I'll see if she's hungry then we'll watch TV. until you get back." "Alright, don't worry about me. Everything will be good. See you later, Tiaja`." Tiaja` said, "See you later Thirsty!" She giggled and they all began to chuckle. Thirst got out and closed the door. He nodded at Destiny and watched as she drove away.

With his hand in his pocket, he drew a deep breath. The cold air caused fog to come from his mouth. From behind, Slice came up. "What's happening Thirst?"

Thirst turned to face Slice. Thirst said, "Let's go inside." They walked towards the café. When they went in, they seated themselves at a booth near the window. A fine, young, black waitress came over and greeted them, placing menus on the table for both of them. She asked, "Can I get you guys some coffee?" Thirst said, "Cappuccino". Slice said, "Make that two."

"Coming right up." The waitress departed as Slice began to speak. "So you finally decided to be a man and earn some real cash!?!"

"Um, it's a good thing you caught me in a good mood Slice, otherwise I would tell you to go to hell! This has nothing to do with me." Slice had a strange look on his face. He was about to say something when the waitress reappeared with the cappuccinos. Slice said to the waitress, "So you like it here?" "It's okay." "Wouldn't you like better than okay? I'm hiring." "No I'm fine. I'll only be here another 8 weeks until I finish my course." "Really." She nodded. Slice went on, "What are you…" "Slice!" Thirst interrupted, "This is important man, we have no time for small talk." Slice nodded in agreement. The waitress asked, "Would you be ordering something to eat?" Thirst said, "No… uh…can we just be alone for a few." She said, "Sure." "Thank you."

Thirst waited until the waitress was

completely gone and he said, "Look, I already told you I'm not getting into that shit anymore. Remember the last time what happened to me. I thought I'd never see the streets, again." "You know how the law is man, they just try to scare you into a snitch, or a bitch. So what category you fall in, Thirst?" "I didn't come here to argue with you. I come here to help your dumb ass." "And how is that?" "They wanna kill you man." "Who?" "I don't know. All I know is, the guy that's in charge, his name is Xavier." "Xavier?" Thirst nodded and Slice looked down, appearing to be in deep thought. Then said, "Wait a minute, now I know who the fuck you talking about. That's the muthafucka that took over Nash's turf. He turned it into a warehouse or something."

Thirst said, "Well, I don't know if you know him, but it sure sounds like the same guy." "So, all this time that's who's been after me?" "And me too, to get at you. And the whole time I thought it was you, until they kidnapped me last night, told me the deal."

Slice was still in thought, he spoke, "Okay, I remember now. I was only a youngster then. My uncle used to work for Nasheed. My uncle had to work long hours protecting the spot because there was feedback, that a muthafucka was gonna try to infiltrate. That same muthafucka knew even if he took over the spot, he couldn't stop Nasheed unless he killed him.

My uncle met Xavier face to face at the spot. Offered him thousands to set Nasheed up. My uncle acted as if it was cool, because he knew if he refused right then, he was dead. My uncle came to see me one day, and he played and wrestled with me, as usual. And I saw something in the collar of his jacket, a tracking device.

Anyway, he disposed it and told me what was going on. He wanted me to learn the streets as well as books. My uncle never helped Xavier find Nasheed. A week later, they found Nasheed and my uncle dead in a Lincoln Town Car, parked by the bay."

"Damn. I don't want them to kill you Slice. That's why I come."

"Hold up." Slice leaned over and searched Thirst's jacket collar, then his shirt, and there it was. Slice pulled it from Thirst's shirt and looked at it in a devastating shock. He slammed both of his hands down on the table hard and stated, "God damn it", and he shot out of the booth. Thirst got up and followed. Slice stepped out of the café onto the sidewalk when shots fired.

The rounds from two machine guns were plunging into Slice's body.

The shots didn't stop until he fell, then the car they were reigning from sped off. Thirst came out slowly, then kneeled down beside Slice until the ambulance arrived. After they place Slice in the vehicle, Thirst walked away with his head down.

Scene 2

After Thirst called Destiny to come pick him up, he, she, and Tiaja` went over to Stacey's house. When they arrived, it was a full house with their parents there and all. Everyone was talking and enjoying the gathering. Thirst pulled Stacey to the side and whispered, "We need to talk." Stacey left the room and Thirst whispered to Destiny,

"Excuse me, dear." Destiny nodded in understanding, but Sheila looked puzzled by all the whispering. Thirst left the room to talk to Stacey. Standing in Stacey's bedroom, she asked, "What is it Thirst?"

"Stacey." Thirst paused, shaking his head and let out a deep breath. "I don't know how you gonna take this because I don't know how much he really meant to you, but I must tell you." Stacey began to look concerned. "What are you talking about Thirst? Who are you talking about?" "It's Slice." "Slice? What's wrong? What's wrong with Slice?"

"He was murdered tonight, Stacey." She screamed, "No!"

She cried and fell down to the floor sobbing, "Oh my God, Thirst. You couldn't have." "What? I didn't kill him." "Well, who did?" "I don't know. Listen, I'll tell you all about it, but you must calm down."

"Calm down! Calm down?" She caught herself for a moment, then drew her breath and said, "Thirst it's not just that I'm so crazy about Slice. It's…I'm pregnant, Thirst." Thirst was astounded. He couldn't imagine Stacey being pregnant, especially from Slice. "You're what?" "I'm pregnant, didn't you hear me?" Sheila said, "Yes I did." "MA!" "It's okay Stacey, you're a grown woman. I just wish you would have told me before you told your 'ole knuckle-head brother here." Sheila smiled at Thirst.

Stacey said, "Ma, he's dead." "Who's dead? Stacey calm down and talk to me."

"Thirst just told me that the father of this child was murdered tonight." Sheila drew a breath and said, "Oh my." She fell down beside Stacey and rocked her in her arms, rocking slightly back and forth. "It's okay baby. God will be with us, God will be with us." James came in the room followed by Keisha, Destiny, Jaq and Tiaja`.

James said, "What's going on? Stacey, you alright?" Sheila said, "She just received some very upsetting news James. Hopefully, you'll be delighted to know that you are soon to be a grandfather."

James was stung for a second. Sheila and Stacey were both looking at him now. Stacey's eyes full of tears. Then it seemed he was the center of attention.
"Well, of course I'm proud.
I'm 54 years old and I finally get to be a grandfather, well, then again I already am, right?" He turned around and picked up Tiaja`, and kissed and played nosey with her. Tiaja` liked that and Thirst seemed to be proud that his father took to Tiaja`, and considered her his granddaughter already. "Son, we're gonna make it all legitimate, too. We'll get her mother to the courthouse with us, and get this all settled."

Stacey was pushing up off the floor and James said, "Stacey, you okay?" "Yes dad, except the fact that I have to make plans to be a single mother."

"Don't worry about that sweetie, you know me and your mother will be there for you every step of the way.

" Stacey came and hugged her father and said "Thanks daddy", and buried her face in his should.   Then they all formed a big family hug. Sheila grabbed Destiny's hand and pulled her into the circle.

Shamika was at her apartment sitting on the couch leaning over towards the coffee table full of balled up papers, dishes, and empty food containers.

She was putting fire to a spoon filled with heroin. Once it turned into it's liquid form, she deposited it into a syringe. She thumped the syringe a few times with her fingers, and leaned back on the couch.

She reached over and grabbed the strap that was sitting on the couch next to her , and tied it tightly around her lower bicep, until she saw her vein slowly rise above her skin's surface. She plunged the syringe deeply into her veins, without stopping, emptied its contents.

She fell back convulsively against the couch. With the needle still stuck in her arm, she began having a seizure.

Her eyes were dilating, and blood shot from the previous nights of no sleep. Her face was pale with ashy lips, and her hair looked soft, but tangled from weeks without combing it. Still shaking, out of control, she began to slobber from her mouth, eyes rolling to the back of its sockets, and passed out. Shamika was dead.

"Now that Slice is out of the way, everything can still go as planned. I will still be looked at as a legal, loyal citizen, while in charge of the entire drug supply in New York, along with what I already maintain in half the country. What do you think about that Gordo?"

Gordo kissed his fingertips, threw out his hand and said, "Splendid, magnificent. I couldn't have a better boss." "Good. I'm glad to hear that you appreciate working for me. And if you keep your nose clean, you'll be successful in this business, too. You know, I didn't want to take over Slices business, I just wanted his business taken elsewhere." " To hell!" Gordo said.

Then Xavier said, "Yeah. Well, now that it's available, what the hell." "I'm a step ahead of you boss. Me and the boys went and checked it out last night. Made sure it was safe for you to go and take a look at it. Had to take out this one bitch, though. Must have been his receptionist.

A real Slice fiend, I tell ya." "What you think?" "That shit is nice boss. He got that shit laid…bitches everywhere. I told 'em to just chill out for a few days,
and they'll be really taken care of financially. Don't really have to worry about 'em just up and leaving, because most of them live there. Nowhere else to go. Single mothers and all. Rooms filled with pussy, weed, coke , heroin, and alcohol." "Umm. I guess I have to go take a look at it tomorrow. See who owns the deed, and maybe make some small changes, huh? Step it up a notch, ha, ha, ha", Xavier chuckled.

He felt terrific, then a buzzer went off in the conference room.
"Boss, the Method's here. He's here to see you.." "The Method?…I thought I told that…" Xavier cut himself off and caught a breath,,
"I'll be right down." Xavier moved quickly to the door and said to Gordo, "Take the rest of the day off, I'll see you tomorrow."
Gordo nodded his head and in a flash, Xavier was out of the room. He walked down the

stairs to the front door.

The walkway to the door was surrounded by elegance. Xavier had taste.

Before he was able to open the front door a voice called out to him from another room, "are you coming back to bed Xavier, I miss you!" "I'll be there in a minute Samarity. I'm busy right now."

Samarity had on only a robe, untied to submerge her nakedness. "But daddy…" "In a minute, I said." Xavier opened the door and shoved the Method back from the entrance way, and closed the door behind him,

"Hey, what the deal man" the Method said. "I told you, you crossed the line the last time and I was gonna spare your life on the account that you'll stay your ass away from here." Xavier drew a 44 magnum from his waistline. "Wait, wait a minute, man. This shit is serious, man." "What? Spit it out!" The Method drew a breath and said, "Listen, you know what I do..I don't" "I said spit it out, goddamn it!" "Okay…okay man, you got me breathing all hard and shit. And get that damn gun out my face.

I can't talk like that. I said this shit was serious…important. Get the damn gun out my face!" Xavier lowered his weapon. "Okay, like I was saying. I don't rap no more. I'm picking up where I left off, without stiffing you this time. "

Xavier took a narrow, piercing look, after the Method made that comment.

"What -is it- Method!?!" "Okay…okay. That nigga Slice, he's dead. Somebody cold smoked his ass last night." "And?"
"And he was rich, you know. I would go get that money myself, but I don't have the manpower." "Nor the brains, So what is it?" " Let's go inside….Let's go inside nigga." Xavier turned around slowly to go inside, the Method followed him and said, "Yeah…yeah."

Stacey called Thirst on his cell phone. When it rung he jumped slightly. He was sitting on the couch next to Destiny. Tiaja` was sleeping on her lap. The lights were dim and they were watching TV. "It hasn't rang in so long I forgot it worked. 'Hello' " "Thirst this is Stacey, I need to speak with you?" "Go ahead, what is it?"

"Can I meet you somewhere? It's important." "Well, I'm at Destiny's right now." "Well, where is that? How do I get there?"

Thirst gave the directions to Stacey then she

said, "I'll be right there." Stacey rushed out of her apartment. She was already dressed. She noticed it was already dark outside when she made it to her car. She got in and drove away.

Gordo got a phone call at his house. "Gordo. I need you to do some work tonight." "Sure, anytime, Xavier." "What did you just call me!?!", "Uh, I'm sorry, my-my, wife's sitting right here," Gordo whispered. More angrily this time Xavier said, "What the fuck did you call me!?!" "Anytime boss, I'm sorry." "Who the fuck is that Gordo? You don't gotta kiss no body's fucking ass to get paid.
You always look out for your fuckin friends more." "Nancy, quiet down." "Put a muzzle on that bitch."

"I'm sorry boss. She doesn't understand." "And she never will. Anyway, get the guys lined up to get the stash out of Slice's suite." "You mean he kept the money in his house?" "That's the word right now.
Crash the whole building if you have to.
    But, avoid it if possible." Gordo listened on the phone for awhile. Nancy was looking at him angrily. He glanced over at her and smiled. She rolled her eyes and turned to face

the TV. "Uh huh. Okay boss." He hung up. "Now what Gordo? Something's not right, here." "Everything's fine honey. I just gotta do a little overtime.

Get us out into a better place. You don't like it here do you?" Nancy shook her head "no", like a little innocent girl. "Then let me do what I gotta do." Gordo stood up and reached for his jacket. Leaned down and gave Nancy a kiss on the forehead.
"I'll be back before midnight." In an instant Gordo left the room. Nancy sat staring at the door for a moment, then grabbed the stuffed teddy bear beside her and threw it at the door. Then began to pout.

Scene 3

The door bell to Destiny's house rang. Thirst looked at Destiny. "I'll get it, I think it might be Stacey." Thirst got up and opened the door, certain it was Stacey, anxious to know what she wanted. "Do you mind going for a ride? I need to speak to you." "Sure Stacey, but hold on a minute." Thirst walked back to the living room where Destiny was. "It's Stacey. She wants me to take a ride with her." "Okay, I'll see you in a little while."

Thirst went over and kissed both Destiny and Tiaja` on the forehead and said, "See you in a little while." Thirst left.

He and Stacey were driving away, when she said, "I'm sorry about dragging you out like this. But it's really important." "It's okay Stacey, what's up?" "Well, me and Slice have been seeing each other for about eight months. I know he wasn't the most trusting guy a girl could have, but he was really, really sweet to me.

 I mean, he was so respectful, and he always tried his best to make me feel special. Well, a few months ago, he told me if anything ever happens to him he was gonna leave some money in his safe for me. He told me not to be bashful, and just go and get it, because I may need it.
Well, I'm still bashful about it all. But, we do need it Thirst. Our parents are out of a home, and I'll be a single mother soon." "Well, just go and get it Stace. What is it? You act like something's wrong with that." "No. It's nothing wrong with it. I'm just scared that's all." "Scared? Why?"

    "Because, he told me to take guns with me." "Hmm, he must have suspected that if he gets killed, they'll be coming for the money, too. Well, where's the guns?" "In the trunk. So, are you coming with me?" "Of course. I just hope it's worth it." "It is. Because I promised him, no matter how much it is… It's worth it to me, Thirst."

    Thirst nodded his head in agreement. "So

where're we going?" "East Manhattan, he has a penthouse there. He has my name down as a frequent visitor, along with the keys, security code, and the combination to the safe."

"Damn!" "What?" "It's just crazy how…I just didn't know that's all." "Well, it's not for you to know all your older sister's personal affairs." "Eh, yuck." She giggled at Thirst, and looked back at the road as she drove on.

Gordo was sitting out in front of the penthouse building in a black Chevy van. The Method was in the passenger's seat and three of the goons were in the back seats. The Method said, "You ready to do this?" Gordo said, "We're always ready. Are you ready?" "You muthafuckin right, what's up?" "UH HUH ,you all know the plan, stick to it…let's go."

They were opening the doors when they saw headlights, then closed them back fast. "Well, well, well, would you look a' here. It's Thirst with some chick.
Seems you were telling the truth after all, 'Messed up'." "You trying to be funny fat boy? The name is Method." The Method put his finger in Gordo's face, "You better watch how you say my name, bitch." Gordo slapped

Method's hand down, and with a sudden reflex Method punched Gordo and dazed him. Gordo shook his head then grabbed his jaw checking for swelling. Then he tossed an evil look at Method, then Method said, "Are you ready- let's go get this money."

Gordo opened the door and the goons seemed to take that as their cue, and they all got out of the van and headed towards the building.

Thirst and Stacey were just walking into the apartment when Stacey keyed in the code to disarm the alarm. Thirst closed the door behind them.

Stacey turned on the lights. Thirst said, "You know where the safe is?" "Yeah." "Well, let's not waist any time here, I'm starting to feel uncomfortable." "Alright…come on."

Downstairs the five were moving swiftly all over the lobby making demands. They began tying up the desk clerks, except for the young lady Method was speaking to. He seemed to be macking to her. One of the goons was choking the security guard with his right arm wrapped around the guard's throat. The guard passed out and the goon pushed him to the floor. Then he took a set of keys from his pocket, then tied him up. All the workers were strangled or tied up.

They put them in the room behind the desk. Then some of the goons took the elevator upstairs.

Stacey said, "Oh my God." Then Thirst said, "that's a lot of freakin' money, man." "What's this?" It was a jewelry box with Stacey's name on it. She opened it up. It was a huge diamond ring inside. The band was made of platinum. It was a small note inside that read, "Will you marry me? I know I gotta change, but please give me a chance." Stacey burst into tears.

Thirst hugged her and said, "Stacey, we gotta go." She nodded her head knowingly, still teary-eyed with her head down. Shortly after, Thirst began the operation.

She started helping him load into bags, the cash from the safe, weighing at about 130 lbs. There were eight duffle bags stored in this large, vault-like safe.

Each duffle bag had wheels, and Thirst and Stacey were loading them fast. When they were done, they were drenched in sweat. Thirst grabbed the AR that was hanging in the safe and hung it around his shoulders. They pulled the bags out of the safe and headed out the door. When they went out into the hallway, one of the goons were checking the locks on one of the apartment doors. Thirst and Stacey tried to sneak over to the elevator.

Once they reached it, they pushed the button and the goon looked up and saw them.

He rushed towards them. The elevator door opened as they struggled with the luggage. He was getting closer. Within five feet now, Thirst decided he should shoot their assailant.

The rifle spit fire as it was penetrating rounds in the chest of the goon. Then he fell to the floor as the elevator door closed, with Stacey and Thirst inside. It was going down to the lobby. Stacey looked nervous, but Thirst began to look like a warrior. Stacey looked up at him and seemed not to recognize him. The elevator came to a halt, but it was not yet the bottom floor. It was the second floor. Thirst began pushing the button for the bottom floor, but the elevator wouldn't move. Then the door slid apart as a large size latino guy came rushing into the elevator to tackle Thirst and Stacey. He wrestled with Thirst in attempt to take the assault rifle from him. Stacey was pounding on his back with all her might, but he pushed her to the floor outside of the elevator. Thirst reached in his waistband for the hand gun he had stored there.

He shot the goon three times until he fell. Thirst said, "Stacey listen to me good, I want you to stay on the elevator with the money!" "What!?!" Stacey said nervously, practically crying.

"Listen, I said stay here for ten minutes and then come down to the lobby. Hold down the close button so the elevator doesn't move or open." "What are you going to do Thirst? How will I know it's going to be safe when I come out?" "I thought I said listen! Now, I have this assault rifle I'm just going to have to kill everyone that looks like a bad guy.

We can make it out of here alive. Now, hopefully the money comes with us, alright!?! Did I make myself clear? Ten minutes, close button."

"Alright be careful, Thirst." "I will." Thirst exited the elevator and the door closed between he and his sister. He saw the goon lying on the floor that he'd shot just recently. He went to scope things out from that floor, to the floor below, which would lead to the lobby. Hopefully, he doesn't have to use the assault rifle for he and his sister to make it out of here.

<u>Scene4</u>

Down in the lobby, Method was talking to the receptionist. "You wanna live luscious, don't make any wrong moves and the ole' Meth dog will make sure you stay safe. If you make any noise... if you even look like you wanna tell somebody...b-loww! You to understand?" The lady nodded her head 'yeah', then Method continued. "Now my boyz are bringin down some major cash. I'll make sure you're taken care of. I'll even take you out to dinner if you like. What... to good for a brother? I'm really nice 'til I...." Method was cut off by a cop entering the building. He was strolling over to the desk.

Method whispered to the girl, "don't make me kill the both of you. I'll do it! The cop said, "what's up Regina, how's it going?" He glanced at Method with an evil look, then looked back at Regina. Regina and Method glanced at each other, then she turned to respond to the cop , "Nothing, I'm doing fine, how are you?"

"Good. Just thought I would stop by and check on you. Never know when a crook might pay a visit. With that remark he looked at Method, again. Method shot him the same evil look. The cop turned back to Regina and said, "you sure you okay?" "Yes I'm fine. Why-why, don't you come back another time? We're having a little family discussion, I guess." "Oh, okay I see, I didn't know you had a brother." "Cousin." "Oh, good to meet you."

The cop reaction Method for a hand shake. Method didn't reach back, he just kept staring at the cop like he wanted to kill him, which he did. "I think I better get going. I'll talk to you later, Regina." "Okay, see-see you…later." Method and Regina stared at each other for a moment. Then Method blurted out, "what the fuck is taken them so long!?!", looking at his watch. Then he pulled out his cell phone, dialed a number and put the phone to his ear.

Scene 5

Thirst was creeping down the stairwell, the loaded rifle in hand. He stopped when he heard a sound. The sound of maybe someone's pants rubbing together, slowly. It had to be a goon. Thirst listened intently. He stood still, except for the moment he had to wipe the sweat from his forehead.

He leaned back against the wall of the stairwell, waiting for the raw appearance of the assailant, as he obviously grew nearer. Steadily, but nervously, Thirst held the rifle up with all his might. Growing increasingly impatient, Thirst shot at the first glimpse of the goon. He missed.

The goon said, "it's all over kid. And look, I'm sorry it had to end this way." Thirst said, "fuck you muthafucka. We're makin' it out of here alive and right now." Thirst let off rounds in the direction of the voice, angrily but suddenly felt stupid, after the fact of wasting shells. "There's no way you're getting out of here alive kid. We got you surrounded." "Fuck you Gordo.... Wait a minute....Gordo? Gordo is that you?" " In the flesh baby. And plan to remain that way. A million dollars richer."

"Why you dirty, double crossing fuck. How could you?" "Hey, money talks, co-workers get killed." At that instant Gordo reached around and took a shot at Thirst. Thirst already prepared to shoot, landed a bullet right in dome of Gordo Vascellez. Thirst crept down the stairs to see if he was really dead.

He said, "Damn", and drew in a deep breath as he symbolized making a trinity cross over his chest, in respect of Gordo's departure.

Thirst exited the stairwell into the lobby. He heard the scream of a woman and angry yells from a man's voice. Then he heard a slap. That's when Thirst snapped. He rushed into the open area of the lobby, rifle aimed steady.

He felt only slightly relieved to see that it wasn't Stacey. The Method shouted, "what you gonna do, muthafucka?" At that instant, a goon came up behind Thirst and started choking him, struggling to take the rifle from his hands.

Method started laughing loudly, like what he was seeing was truly hilarious.

Thirst struggled hard, biting the goon's arm and taking his elbow to the goon's gut. The goon let go and hit Thirst with a hard blow to the back of the head. Thirst went down, but his name said it all at this point. He had a thirst to make sure he and his sister make it out of here alive. On his back, he quickly and relentlessly aimed the rifle at the goon, who was in the process of pouncing on top of him. Squeezing the trigger 'til he nearly unloaded the banana clip. The goon fell to the floor, dead before he made contact with it. Thirst stood up facing Method, who had his arm around the neck of the young lady. Method said, "yeah boy, what you gonna do now. I'll kill this bitch." Thirst couldn't believe he was about to say this. He prayed it would work. "So what, kill her. I don't know that bitch.
You can kill her, fuck her, whatever, I don't

give a shit. You keep standing there like that, I'm a kill both of you. Justifiable muthafucka."

Method pushed the woman to the floor and said, " I think I'll fuck her, and you too, bitch." He shot, Thirst shot back as Method dropped behind the desk. "God damn it son, you almost shot me.

Ha, ha, ha." Stacey came out of the elevator. "Thirst." "No, Stacey get down," she didn't understand, she just stood. In a flash, shots sounded off and Stacey went down. Thirst yelled, "No, Stacey please." He ran to his sister looking over his shoulder.
Nothing from Method, no sight of him.
Stacey mumbled, "I'm okay Thirst, I'm okay. Protect yourself." "No Stacey, I can't leave you." "I'm serious Thirst, I'm okay.
I got hit in the shoulder, it just burns that's all. And I'm a little woozy. Just get us out of here, bro."

"Okay sis, I love you." "I love you too."
Then Method said, "you ready to die too, man. You better sure hope you are."

Thirst loaded the rifle with another clip, and started ripping up the front desk with rounds from the A.R., while walking towards it. Method said lowly to himself, "oh my fuckin god, the kids gone wild."

He tried to crawl around the desk to get away. Thirst came up behind him. "Talk that shit now boy." Method started to run. Thirst began to chase him. With the option to shoot em' in the back, Thirst let him flee. Then he went back for his sister. "Stacey, Stacey, you alright?" "Yeah".
She was raising herself up off the floor. Thirst began to help her. Then they heard sirens.

"Oh no Stacey, we gotta get back up to the apartment for a while, or they gonna think we in on some kind of drug war." "Okay, let's go." They hustled the luggage and things all the way back up to Slice's apartment. Once they made it up, Thirst said, "let's just clean up real good, I'll wipe my prints from this gun, and we're out, okay?" "Okay bro, sounds like a plan"

They were rushing to get organized, so they could finally get away from this place. Thirst put on a nice suit from Slice's closet. Stacey put on some clothes she had left there previously, when Slice was alive. She had her shoulder wrapped in bandages so she had to wear something with sleeves to avoid any type of questioning. But, that was apparently an unworldly idea.

One cop stopped them as soon as they exited the elevator into the lobby.
"Excuse me, I'm sorry to bother you, but do you folks live here, in this building?" Thirst said, "yes, well, she does…. or use to. I'm just helping her move." "Did you happen to see or hear anything, in regards of this tragic event?" "No, I'm afraid not. I did hear strange noises like gunshots, but we assumed it was coming from outside."

"In this neighborhood sir?"
"Hey, I'm sorry. I grew up in the hood. I take it like anything can go down anywhere… 'uh, uh.' (Thirst cleared his throat) as we can see."

"Right…. I hope I didn't take up too much of your time." Thirst and Stacey began to walk rather quickly until they reached their car. They crossed the street with the luggage. Once they reached the car, Method popped up from behind it with his gun aimed at Thirst.

Thirst dropped the bags and turned to face Stacey, shielding her from the danger of getting shot again. Method shot him in his upper back. Thirst yelled. Then the officers outside began to yell, "hey." Method ran off. The cops walked over to Stacey and Thirst, "are you two alright, what happened?" "That guy tried to mug us. We're okay though, just ready to get to my Destiny. I mean, my destination."

"Okay, you don't wanna file a report...... hold on."

The cop listened to his radio. It said, "we were in pursuit of the suspect, when he turned around firing shots at us. He was taken down, call the morgue." "Well, no need. You're safe to go now."

Thirst said, "thank you, thank you very much." Thirst packed the trunk quickly with the luggage, then they got into the Altima. Thirst wasn't bleeding that much, but it did hurt, extremely. Stacey asked, "are you o.k. bro.?" "Yeah, just get me back to Tiaja` and Destiny." "O.k. And in case you don't know bro., you're getting half this money." "No, Stacey. It was my pleasure helping you out. I don't want half of your money." "Thirst, you deserve it more than I do. You saved our asses backed there. Plus you have Tiaja` now."

"Wow Stace. You're the greatest sis." He leaned over and gave her a kiss on the forehead. "You just wowed me, too. Thank you." They laughed. "If it wasn't for the fact I've been shot before, I'd probably be panicking right now."

"Well, this is my first time, so believe me, I'm going straight to the hospital after I drop you off." "I'll be there to see you. I just want to let Destiny and Tiaja` know we're o.k. Dest will be my doctor."

"Huh." Stacey drove as fast as she could without drawing the attention of the N.Y.P.D. they were almost to Destiny's house. Thirst began to laugh, "oh my God…this shit is great!!"

Scene 6

Back at Xavier's place, he was talking to one of his men. "That fucking bastard Method was supposed to call me almost an half an hour ago." He dialed a number on his cordless phone. Apparently, he didn't get a response because he hung up the phone saying,
"I know damn well those idiots didn't mess up forty million fuckin' dollars, cash! If they did, and they're not dead, I'm going to kill them myself...starting with you, if you don't hurry up and get down and let me know what's up." "Yes sir, boss. Right away, sir." The man left immediately out of the room. Xavier went to his bar and poured himself a drink. Took a sip, then slammed the glass down. Scotch

splashed from the glass and it flew everywhere.

Back at the 23rd, Van damage and three other guys were standing around a fire blazing barrel. It was pretty, windy out. The smoke blew laboriously through the dense air. They were drinking cognac straight from their bottles.

Damage said, "much respect to my nigga Slice".

The other guys said, "yeah, yeah, no doubt kid….yeah that's real." They poured to the ground some of their liquor from the bottles. Damage continued, "they'll never be another like him. And I bet those fuckaz gonna try to come take over the spot, now that they took his life. But, I'm telling' you…those bitches got another thing coming to 'em…relentlessly. It's gonna be in reality, hell-on-earth."

"I'll take one to the head to that, Damage. Behind you one hundred, my nigga." Another of the guys said, "what you gonna do about the Kitty Kat?" "Did you hear anything I said? They'll be no muthafucka like Slice around here. I gave the girls their walking papers. They won't be without a place. Those whores pockets fatter than mine," " They must have major dough then."

"Get the fuck out of here Freeze. New York's craziest stick up kid, and you talkin bout I got dough." They all began to laugh. "But yo, on the real Damage, you need us to do anything? I already told you, I'm wit you." " Nah money, I got it all under control. Ya'll lil niggaz just stay out of my way.

You know Damage been doing things on his own for along time now. I tell you what, you tell Sha`mya to give me a holla and I'll throw you some weight."

"Man I already tried to hook ya'll up. She like them young niggaz though. That shit turn her on seeing lil niggaz my age with major bread. I don't know man, I'll tell her though." "Yeah, do that" " No doubt Damage, man . Me and my niggaz man, we bout to raise up out of here, you know. Gotta get up off these bags before dinner gets too cold. We'll holla D."

"Yeah." They slapped knuckles with a finger snap. And Damage watched them run off in the darkness.

"Ahhhh." "I got it. All that moving I'm surprise I got it out so quick honey."
" Thank you Dest. I'm such a baby, huh?" " Yeah, but you're my baby." She glanced at Tiaja` and winked an eye. "Well, my big baby.

Now what's it you want to tell me?"

" You don't have to work anymore." "What are you talking about, Thirst?" "I'm talking about we're rich and you don't want you to work." " And what makes us rich all of a sudden?" "How about $20 million Stacey just given me." "You've got to be kidding, Thirst. Twenty million dollars! Oh my god.
What are we going to do?" " Let's say live good?" " Well, I don't know Thirst."
"You don't have to worry. I know what you're thinking, Destiny." "Yes, Thirst?" "Will you marry me?" "Yes Thirst, oh my god yes."
They hugged each other tightly. Tiaja` was smiling at them. Then she dropped her toy. " Oh, I'm sorry Tiaja`. Your daddy come and take all your attention away. Come here."
Thirst said, "Daddy, wow that sounds nice. Mommy? What you think about that?"

"Yes Thirst. But after we are married. Okay?" They began hugging again. Destiny leaned back with her arms still around Thirst and looked him directly in the eyes. "I just wanna know one thing, do you have anything against going to church and praising the Lord sometimes?" "No Destiny, not at all. I just feel it's not as wholesome as it should be these days.

Now days people think you're going to church to impress somebody. So I stay at home sometimes and watch it on B.E.T. Get real interested, too." Destiny laughed.

"For real baby. I grew up going to church. My mom always said I use to seem very excited to go. I don't remember, but I'm thinking I was just a kid.
I didn't comprehend God all that much. Maybe I was happy cause I was dressed up looking sharp."

"Thirst you're so crazy, I love you. "Wow, I love you too."

Heaven4 some Hell 4Most

Chapter 4
Scene 1

      Back at Xavier's mansion the next day one of the men was tapping at his bedroom door. Xavier opened it and said, "what is it?" "I checked on Gordo and the others like you said , Gordo is dead. All of them are dead." " Where's the money?" "I don't know boss. Seems it was all taken from the safe." " God damn it. Did you go by the 23rd?" "Yes sir. I didn't see anyone though. I guess the girls went on break. Ha, ha, ha." Xavier said, "something's funny!" The man straightened his face quickly. "No sir boss, I'm sorry sir."

"Get all the boys up, and pull the limo out front. I wanna go check it out." "Yes sir." He went to go do as he was told and Xavier closed his room door shut.

Damage was in the Kitty Kat building. Everyone was gone except for a few junkies laying on the floor, in a zone. They seemed completely oblivious to Damage being there until he said, "unless you muthafuckaz are ready to die, I suggest you get the hell out of here. You see this? Yeah, explosives nigga. This shit is bout to blow…. Alright take it for a joke nigga, your ass ain't gonna ever see no type of dope again bitch. Sit there!" With that the fiends got up slowly and left the building Damage had to laugh to himself. "Dumb muthafuckaz don't even realize they'll be better off blowing up in this muthafucka." Damage set the explosives up all over the building, then went out the back.

Thirst, Destiny, and Tiaja` was cruising the Hudson on the ferry. Destiny said, "I've got to be the most luckiest woman in the world. I knew there was something about you, since the first moment I laid eyes on you. I mean, you're so blessed, and I just feel blessed being around you.

Like ever since you came into my life, everything just seemed more beautiful and beautiful each day. And we have this gorgeous little girl with us.

I got you, and with all this money, we don't have to ever worry about if we can take care of Tiaja`, now.
And we never have to spend too much time apart." "That's exactly what I was thinking. I love you Destiny." "I love you too, Travis Ramone Thurston." They hugged, and Destiny whispered, "thank you God." Tears falling from her eyes, she began to smile. She was so happy, and Thirst was too. Tiaja` was hugging Thirst around his leg as they looked out into the river. It seemed like a very beautiful moment. The weather felt nice. The sky was a little hazy, but plenty of sun. Seagulls were scouring, diving in and out of the water, hunting for food. It looked like paradise.

<u>Scene 2</u>

Back at Stacey's house, the family was finishing up breakfast Jaq said, " Stacey I want a dog." "You want a dog?" "Yes." "Okay you can have a dog." Keisha said, "I want a diamond ring." Stacey said, "sure sis, no problem." Then Keisha and Jaq giggled . Sheila said, "Don't go spoiling your brother and sister, Stacey."

"Why not mom, there's plenty." "Because they're going to have to continue to be humble and courteous children, that's why." "They could still be that. Do you two promise to continue to be humble, courteous, little rich kids?" "Stacey stop it." Shelia got up from the table and went into the living room. Stacey said, "mom."

James said, "it's okay Stacey, let her calm down., she's just unsure. I mean from rags to riches over night." " Yeah, I understand. I realize there's problems with having money, too. Probably more than without. But I'm still overtaken by this unrelenting feeling that I rather not be without.

Why mom's gotta be so old fashion?" Then the doorbell rang. From the other room Shelia yelled, "I heard that Stacey. I'll get the door. Oh son, are you okay?" "Yes mom, I'm fine." "Oh my God, Stacey told me everything. You're crazy you hear me. The both of you, you two should've known better than to mess around with that drug money like that."

"But mom…." "No, I don't need to hear it. I've talked to Stacey and I do somewhat understand. But, you could've gotten yourselves killed.

And besides, how do you expect us to spend that kind of money without the government getting involved, huh?" Destiny and Thirst looked at each other. "Well mom, Destiny gave me the idea of spending a small amount to start a business. We'll continue renting an apartment and claim a certain amount of taxes from our business to legitimize our profits.

Face it momma, we're not turning the money in. And even better, my parents don't have to struggle no more."

" I don't know son. I just don't know." She smiled and said, "I guess we'll see. Talk to your father about it. See what he has to say." James Thurston yelled from the other room, "I think it's a great idea son..... Honey?" Shelia looked back and gave her husband an evil eye as he entered the living room. "Come on Shelia, lighten up sweetheart. We have got it made!" James did a little shimmy as Shelia cracked a slight grin, still uneasy about all this . She said, "whatever." They all sat down to watch TV. Shelia said, "Tiaja honey, come here to grandma. Come give me a hug." Tiaja ran and jumped into her grandmother's arms and began laughing and squirming when her grandmother started playing with her.

Thirst said, "how are you feeling Stacey?" " Lavish darling, just marvelous." " I mean your shoulder crazy?" "Never felt better kid", she said while fanning her shoulder with about ten one hundred dollar bills. They started laughing .

SCENE 3

At the Kitty Kat, Xavier was stepping out the back of his limo looking around, and observing the area . He moved away from the vehicle and the driver closed the door behind him. Two other gentlemen from the limo walk up beside him and the three of them headed towards the building.

Once they entered Xavier asked, "Where is everyone?" " Huh, I think they may... be... upstairs boss." " Come on, lead the way." They started up the stairs. "Yeah, I think I can do something with this. What am I talking about? I know I can."

He managed a grin, but couldn't help the uneasiness he felt being here. What could it be, he thought. He looked around cautiously. He saw something that curiously caught his eye. There was exposed wire going along the wall.

It lead from upstairs to downstairs.

"What is this?" Then he saw the bomb. "It's a trap, let's get out of here."

But, it was too late. Outside Damage was standing on the sidewalk with a detonator in hand. He pushed the button and a loud boom came from inside the building. Fire and smoke shot through the windows, and the walls began to crumble. Damage laughed out loud. "That your ass boy, yeah…"

Then Damage fled the scene.

Scene 4

Thirst figured a lot of the money should go to charity, being that just a couple of million dollars would last them a lifetime. Shelia said, " Oh yes Thirst, that's a great idea." Thirst said "I know, but not all at once. I want to be sure those people that suppose to be helping sick and abused children and women, and even the homeless, are going to use it specifically for that. I want to see them expand their services and then I'll start my own private facility to aid those in need. That way I'll receive funding from the government, and send that money to aid the ones helping control diseases and hunger in Africa."

"James do you hear our son?" " Yep, that's my

boy. My main man that is." Stacey asked, "mom should I mange the money for you and dad, or can you handle all this at once?"

Shelia said, "all what?" "Five million." "Oh no honey, I don't have the slightest idea what to do with all that. You keep it." "Come on momma, this isn't "Goodtimes", and you're not Florida Evans."

"Excuse me?" "Just joking momma, I mean just take it." "No. I'm not trying to be rude, I just wouldn't know what to do with it. Just get us some place to stay, and transportation. And nothing fancy."

"Okay momma, love you." "Love you too, sweetheart." At that moment, a breaking news flash came across the screen.

"Reporting live from W. 23rd street, there has been a very tragic event. This building here has just exploded moments ago, and it appears that bodies have been found inside."

Thirst said, "Hey that's Slice's old spot isn't it? Ah man. Wait a minute, that's the limo those bad guys kidnapped me in. Tell me it's them, please, please." Thirst's mom said, "Thirst, what are you saying? You're not suppose to wish death on anyone." "Mom, you don't understand. They tried to kill me and Stacey. And probably would've came for us

being that we got away with Slice's money."
Thirst's mom said, "please let it be them lord,
please, please, please."
Thirst said, "I'm going to go check it out. I'll
be right back." He gave everyone a kiss, and
shook his brother and his dad's hand. His dad
gripped his hand and said, "You're gonna be
alright, son?"

"Yes pop, I'm good." Destiny said, "you
want me to come with you, baby?" "No baby,
I'll be alright." "Here, take my truck."

"No, I'm going to walk. I could move better
on foot. Besides I need the air and the exercise.
See you in a bit." Thirst dashed out the door,
and ran up the block. He was breathing hard,
so he slowed down to a fast walk. He began to
think to himself about all the things he went
through these past few days. Some of the
things made him sad, but most of all, he was
happy. His family was alive and in good
health. He met the most perfect woman in the
world to him.
He also had more money than he ever dreamed
or even wished for.

He was straight. He stopped for a moment
and thought aloud. "Too bad anybody had to
die for me to get here. I guess I had to take 'em
out...cause they sure as hell was gonna take

me out.

Epilogue

"Never thought life could be so good."
"Yeah, your boy blessed us decent, baby....
I'm 'bout to go downstairs, fix me a drink.
You want something, boo?" "Yeah, bring me
shot of that henny on the rocks, wit yo sexy
ass." She giggled at his comment then said,
"gotta keep this ass right for you papi. You
make me feel so good..."

With that Sha`mya stepped towards the door
to exit the room. She had an attractive
demeanor. She was topless, with a g-string and
stilettos on. She was built like a goddess.
Thick ass switching from left to right. Damage
had it made for sure. He bought about six acres
of land with the money Thirst had given him.

They kept in contact through Stacey, who also gave Damage a nice sum of money for his good deeds.

Though Damage had wifey and kids at his other home, he couldn't resist breaking in his new home with a nice, young piece of hot ass. When wifey moves in, Damage wouldn't think of fucking another woman in this bed.
Or this house even. "Start the Jacuzzi for me, baby."

Damage yelled to Sha`mya, as he heard her coming up the stairs. "Hell yeah, baby. You finally decided to listen to me and get up out of bed." "Yeah, well this shit is cozy. Besides, I'm enjoying acting like a nigga that ain't never had shit. Damn, I almost forgot... I don't have to hustle no more. Ha, ha. Yeah."

"You may now, kiss the bride." He removed the veil from Destiny's face, and gave her a long passionate kiss. Everyone in the church cheered loudly. Thirst swept Destiny from her feet, and carried her out of the church and into their limousine, waiting out front. Little kids were blowing bubbles at them, in commemoration of their marriage. Sheila Thurston was teary-eyed. James was smiling widely. Some of Destiny's family was there, but her parents had died when she was young. Her parents were attacked by a stick-up kid in Harlem. They were suspected to be drug dealers, so the kid thought they had money on them.

Thirst and Destiny were off to their honeymoon in Paris, France. Their next stop, they planned to return for Tiaja` and go to Mexico.

James and Sheila were hugging, watching their son and daughter in-law ride away in the limo. Tiaja` stood in front of them watching, also. Keisha stood next to her mother, and Jaq stood next to his father.

Jaq and Keisha enjoyed having Tiaja` around. They played games and went swimming out back of the Thurston's mini-mansion.

"Hello, Mom, come quick! I think it's time! The paramedics are already on their way to come pick me up. Hurry, ma!"

"James! Stacey's about to have the baby! Let's go!" They rounded up the children and were off to see Stacey have her first child. They all arrived at the hospital in just enough time to see the baby boy exit the womb, of Stacey Thurston. The five of them had to put on a special gown and mask to enter the room. Sheila asked, "so what're you naming him?"

Stacey said, "Devin Dumas jr."

Since Xavier died without a living will, the mansion was turned over to Samarity, being it was her legal residence for the past six years. She began dating Johnnie. Better known as the warehouse supervisor. Every night, she and Johnnie would get high on coke. She'd found it in the walls in the basement.
Not including the vast amount Johnnie had taken from the warehouse.

Most of the time they partied alone. But, this particular night they had guest. They called it a "swap party". Each couple would take turns having sex with each others girlfriend or spouse. Samarity sprinkled cocaine all over Johnnie's dick, and watched the other man's wife suck it off.

At the same time, the husband was behind Samarity fucking her in the ass, with his dick covered in coke. They had so much blow, they had literally bathed in it.

Preoccupied with partying all the time, there was never anytime for thought of the outside world. The next night, the same four guest came over. They felt a little uneasy because there was no electric working in the home. Now, word on the streets, this is the first mansion ever known in history, to have its electric disconnected due to non-payment.

Tasha Patterson finally decided to call Keisha, and let her know what's been going on with her. "Girl where have you been? I've been worried sick. Rumor has it you…" "Keisha, just listen. You know I ain't big on rumors, so just hear the truth straight from me." Keisha listened intently.

She hadn't heard from her best friend since the accident, a year ago. Apparently, she'd dropped out of school and ran away from home. "I don't have much time, I'm just calling to say I do love you and I miss you." "Girl, I love you too, where have you been?" "I couldn't stand going back to school looking like this. My parents were trying to force me, so I jetted." "Looking like what? What are you talking about, Tasha?" "The accident ruined my face."

"NO!"

"So, I decided to choose a different way to live." "A different way to live? Tasha, you're only sixteen. And I'm sure your parents miss you like crazy. Come on girl, use your head. I know your parents can work something out. You gotta give them a chance." "Yeah, well I've been through a lot since I've been out here. I've changed a lot. My parents wouldn't want me around now."

"You can't be serious. I know Mr. and Mrs. Patterson will always love YOU, no matter what." "You think so?" "Honey boo, I know so." They giggled at that, then Tasha said, "I miss you so much Keish." "I miss you too, girl. Now go home before I get upset with you."

"...Hey, Keish?" "Yes Tosh." "Where did you all move to!?! I've been needing to talk to you. I just now found your number in the directory. These streets have been crazy- rough on me. I don't want to go home yet. I need to tell you something. Can I come over?"
"Of course, girl. I'll have my dad take me to come pick you up. Where are you?" "I can't believe your ass is here in my studio, talkin' bout you wanna cut a track. What's really going on, Van Damage?"

Damage responds through the mic, "Nothing major, Mix. I feel I gotta cut one for my nigga Slice. **And** that nigga Thirst. You know he be holding it down, keeping' it real G, too. Both them niggaz got me where I'm at today. So all due respect, I want you to drop that mufuckin' beat my nigga was working on before he'd passed the mic for good; and let me show the world what it is to survive in the hood, when you got envy, hate, drugs, and poverty in the mufuckin' hood." Mix started the beat as Damage began bobbing his head, focused so he can began rapping on the right bar. Mix pointed at Damage as his cue to start spitting the lyrics.

"You gotta heat em up/

when they just like you/

you gotta heat em up/

when they don't-give a fuck-like you/

 you gotta heat em up/

they'll kill your wife-and your bit-ches too/

heat them muthafuckaz up-before they heat up

you………"

This is a sensational, yet inspirational

Developed from life's logical, yet actual

A message to be fundamentally
    Implemented into text

People I love like the days

Though no day's the same

But one in the same through structure

Don't seek fault in another

Only peace within can alleviate stress

-BRP

www.ingramcontent.com/pod-product-compliance
Lightning Source LLC
Chambersburg PA
CBHW070634030426
42337CB00020B/4004